Fine-art Weaving

Fine-art Weaving

A study of the work of Artist-Weavers in Britain

Irene Waller

B.T. Batsford Ltd   London
Van Nostrand Reinhold   Australia Melbourne

By the same author

Thread an Art Form
Tatting a Contemporary Art Form
Knots and Netting
The Craft of Weaving
Textile Sculptures
Design Sources for the Fibre Artist

ISBN 0 7134 0412 4 (U.K.)
ISBN 0 442 25003 7 (Australia)
Filmset in 'Monophoto' Apollo by
Servis Filmsetting Ltd, Manchester

Printed in Great Britain by
The Anchor Press Ltd, Tiptree, Essex
for the publishers B.T. Batsford Ltd
4 Fitzhardinge Street London W1H 0AH
and Van Nostrand Reinhold
17 Queen Street Mitcham Victoria 3132

Contents

Introduction *6*

SECTION 1 **Recent Developments in Handweaving in Britain** *7*

SECTION 2 **The Work of 17 British Artist-weavers** *22*

Tadek Beutlich *22*

Archie Brennan *30*

Geraldine Brock *38*

Peter Collingwood *42*

Bobbie Cox *50*

Fionna Geddes *56*

Myriam Gilby *60*

Maureen Hodge *66*

Robert Mabon *72*

Fiona Mathison *78*

Kathleen McFarlane *84*

Theo Moorman *90*

Alec Pearson *96*

Maggie Riegler *102*

Sax Shaw *110*

Unn Sönju *114*

Ann Sutton *120*

SECTION 3 **Studio Addresses, Exhibitions, Commissions and Collections** *128*

Bibliography *141*

Photograph Acknowledgments *142*

Index *143*

Introduction

Of late, the world-wide Fibre Art movement, in which great artists are making statements through the media of fibres, yarns and textile-based techniques, has been the subject of several important books. It seemed, therefore, the time to look at the scene in Britain, where seminal work goes on both in the studios of individual artists and within the various art institutions.

This book looks at the work of 17 artist-weavers working in Britain. Tadek Beutlich has been included, for, although he now lives in Spain, most of the creative working years of his life were spent in Britain and he is an indissoluble part of any consideration or appraisal of weaving in Britain. The word 'weavers', used here, must be taken in its widest sense to denote designers of textile constructions – who, somewhere along the line, are of course firmly weave-based with all the disciplines and creative opportunities that weaving offers.

The first section of the book traces the development of handweaving and its allied arts in Britain during the last 50 years. The second section then looks in detail at the work of some of today's greatest exponents. The third section comprises a reference list of their exhibitions and commissions, and gives their studio addresses. (Visitors are generally welcome to studios – but never without appointment.)

There is so much to learn from what these artists have to say and how they say it, both artistically and technically, that the beginner and the experienced weaver can both benefit from studying their work. It is also of great interest that there is such strong individuality of approach within a comparatively small geographical area as the British Isles.

There is Peter Collingwood, once a medical practitioner, living in a Victorian schoolhouse in flat, misty Suffolk, and producing his elegant, controlled, linear thread organizations; Archie Brennan in granite Edinburgh, linking the best of traditional and contemporary flat tapestry with masterly graphic imagery; Ann Sutton in Dorset producing knitted three-dimensionalities which lie somewhere between sculpture and furniture; Theo Moorman in a Cotswold village, weaving her delicate, subtle images of rocks and stones; Maureen Hodge, also in Edinburgh, giving life to her lyrical, poetic, mystical dreams through the medium of three-dimensionalized flat tapestry; and Kathleen McFarlane in the watery plains of Norfolk, creating violent three-dimensional sisal statements about life's organic beauty. Each artist is quite individual, even though, in terms of location, culture and media, they are all in such close proximity.

It is certain that much is due, directly or indirectly, to the fine, basic work that has been embedded in both art and craft training in Britain. As a nation, and the initiators of the Industrial Revolution, the British have always been both creative and inventive and yet, at the same time, by virtue of their own inventions, had their feet held firmly on the ground. The links between industry and art are invaluable and have made British craftsmen what they are.

Recent Developments in Handweaving in Britain

A point of reference

The period of the Second World War, 1939–45, is a useful date from which to make an assessment of some of the developments in the history of handweaving in Britain which have contributed to the particular aspect of the subject dealt with in this book, namely the use of fibre, yarn and textile constructions, not as yardage, but to an expressionist end. From that point (a vast gash in time and experience) one can look back a little, but mostly forward as it proved to be a watershed of a sort, after which the move to the present situation gained momentum.

The Industrial Revolution

Looking back as far as the eighteenth and nineteenth centuries, it would seem that the Industrial Revolution in Britain not only brought the country immense prosperity but also did it certain irreparable damages. One of these was to cripple the valid and proper use of hand processes in the production of goods. The machine became dictator and innumerable existing social institutions were swept away as irrelevant. All available labour was sucked into the factories and the towns.

The Midlands of England, where the Industrial Revolution took a strong hold in the 1830s, and other similar areas of Britain were swiftly and arbitrarily given over to the demands of machine production, and its people became the drudges of the technological age.

William Morris (1834–96)

William Morris, the great visionary, craftsman and architect of change, was the most vociferous and effective element in establishing a communal effort to bring back balance and reason to the sphere of design. For design had run wild in an excess of decorative vulgarity, so easy was it to embellish manufactured articles. The effort Morris envisaged had to be made by the artists, one of the few groups of people which were outside the maelstrom of dust, sweat and smoke. He advocated that in order to regain equilibrium and to go forward with dignity, it was first necessary to look back to the past. The elements of good craftsman-ship and respect for materials that had existed before the Industrial Revolution were to be melded with the facilities of the new machines, to achieve aesthetically well-designed goods with speed and economy of production.

However, even though Morris's teaching spread fairly rapidly, the use of the machine by man to produce well constructed and aesthetically desirable goods was still not attained for a considerable time. Instead, fine hand-crafted artefacts were the immediate result – jewellery, ceramics, furniture, glass and textiles. From our point of view today, these artefacts seem perhaps slightly self-conscious, but their precious isolated beauty was a positive reaction from the frightful design excesses of the day and the brutal misuse of materials by the manufacturers. Nevertheless, this was hardly design for the people. In time, however, the work of artists, craftsmen and designers wholly influenced by Morris eventually achieved the desired result, and the machine was finally brought under control to produce technically skilful, aesthetically pleasing and contemporarily valid products.

The early twentieth century

In the sphere purely of hand-production, however, the movement started by Morris gradually lost its force, even though the establishment of the Arts and Crafts movement in 1861, and the holding of the first Art and Craft Exhibition in 1888 did much to improve the status of the artist craftsman. The whole movement had been a violent and fervid reaction to a traumatic upheaval in the structure of society and the function of people. The message to be learnt was that it was essential to place man and machine into a relationship where the machine would enrich man's life on both a practical and aesthetic level, rather than denigrate his existence and his values. The handweaver, like others, had played a relevant part in the process, but designing had been carried out in a graphic manner, in the case of textiles, on paper, and the art of handweaving as it had been known almost came to an end, except in the enclaves of firms like Warners of Braintree, who continued to handweave the fine silk brocades and velvets which the machine was too swift and clumsy to accomplish.

Then in the 1920s and 1930s came a handweaving revival, but this time of a different nature. Ideas and influences were filtering through from Scandinavia and from Europe, and these were strongly reflected in the arts and crafts of the period.

In Scandinavia, where the traditional arts and crafts had followed a more continuous and less volatile path, superb examples of individual craftwork were being made. Märta Måås-Fjetterström, in Sweden, was producing fine rugs, furnishing fabrics and wallhangings showing all the strength of tradition melded with contemporary thought, methods and materials. Swedish studios, quantity production and design training were all strongly linked. Eva Antilla, in Finland, was producing delicately envisaged rugs and wallhangings, often based on human or natural form. Scandinavian hand-produced items of glass, ceramics and textiles were almost indistinguishable from commercially made goods; both were totally contemporary in feeling, and yet firmly rooted in unbroken artistic and craft traditions.

In Europe in 1919 the German Bauhaus was created. The word 'Bauhaus' like 'Morris' reverberates again and again, even in the ears of the uninvolved, as being synonymous with seminal and cataclysmic happenings in the art and design world.

The Bauhaus weaving school was set up under the artistic supervision first of Johannes Itten, the painter, and then of Paul Klee. It held (finally) that the handloom itself was a robust and valid design tool, as valid as the painter's brush and canvas, but that the user must be in the mainstream of contemporary artistic thought to achieve designation as an artist, not simply standing on the sidelines nor in any cosy therapeutic backwater. The weaver's materials and tools should be used with respect and craftsmanship but also used both experimentally and seminally, without the inhibitions which the concept of the power-loom can sometimes create. Textile materials, whether natural or synthetic, should be used with care, sensitivity and robustness. The products of the handloom could be equally valid whether yardage or one-off art objects (in which case the weaver would enter unequivocally into the art world, with all which that implies), or as pilot weaves for eventual mass-production.

The firm of Heals in London, for whom Theo Moorman worked between 1930 and 1932, was foremost in the promotion of the new design theories derived from the Continent, as also were Liberty & Co. of Regent Street and the small Primavera Gallery, then in Sloane Street, now in Cambridge. Rugs were a particularly fluid vehicle for artist-weavers' concepts as pattern-repeat was not an inhibiting factor. Rug weaver-designers of distinction were Marion Dorn, (who also designed Jacquard fabrics for Warners), Marion Pepler and Ronald Grierson. Thus the seeds of post-war experiment in Britain were being sown well before the war. The really great designers were absorbing the outside influences with skill and artistry and, in turn, making design statements entirely of their own. However, the Scandinavian influence had a slightly unfortunate side effect. Handweaving also became an 'arty' pastime. The overshot weaves, like the 'Rosepath' and 'Honeysuckle' patterns and their derivatives, were taken up and copied *ad infinitum*. In the hands of the semi-skilled and without true conviction, the results were dull. Yarns used were often plain spinnings and of drab colours: creams, browns, mud-greens and terra-cotta. This image, in turn, was sometimes projected back into industry, particularly in the production of low-quality furnishing yardage where brown, orange and natural 'folk-weave' was considered by some to encapsulate 'good taste'. However, strong forces emerged to combat this trend, and one of the strongest arose in the person of Ethel Mairet.

Ethel Mairet (1872–1952)

Ethel Mairet was a positive, unique and seminal influence on British weaving, and her vigorous spirit and fresh insights into the widest applications of hand-weaving to contemporary life have left an indelible mark.

She was born of a Devon family named Partridge in 1872 and was, from the first, a strong and forceful personality, determined to pursue her life-interests (in her youth, geology) as far as she could, even though, at that time, opportunities for a woman were severely limited. Marriage took her to Ceylon (Sri Lanka) and there she became absorbed in the folk arts and crafts of the native people, particularly in the field of textiles, and particularly in dyeing and spinning. After her return to England, and her separation from her husband, she decided to live at Shottery in Warwickshire, largely because there was a craftsman there who could teach her to dye, spin and weave properly. Eventually she established her own weave studio.

In 1913 she married Philip Mairet, a man interested in the crafts from a social and philosophic standpoint. Together they moved to Ditchling in Sussex to be near the group of artists and craftsmen who had gathered around the calligrapher and illustrator, Eric Gill. The Mairets built a house called 'Gospels', which was to be a place of study and pilgrimage for many craftsmen, but particularly weavers, and until Ethel Mairet's death in 1952, pupils came to her from all over the world.

She herself had received a sparse technical training, but, sparked off by her early interest in geology, and greatly influenced by the rich, colourful folk art of India, she became an original and creative master of spinning and natural dyeing. When her interest had progressed to weaving, she pursued particularly the development of texture as an outcome of experiment on the loom (as was happening in the Bauhaus and Scandinavia) with a variety of fancy spun yarns and clean colours. The new and original yarns she used were designed and produced by Greggs, the yarn-spinners of Stockport, and were to influence whole decades of handweavers and designers of cloth for industry: slubs, knops, gimps, yarns in which natural fibres were often blended with the new man-made or metal yarns or cellophane. Her weaves were basic in concept, like gauze (leno), hopsack, honeycomb or spaced threads, but absolutely new and fresh in her interpretation of them in terms of colour, interest of yarns and originality of sett. All her fabrics were, without exception, a sensual joy to look at and to touch, completely 'of the time' and totally original.

Fortunate were those who could study with her at 'Gospels', 'could' being the operative word as she was a demanding teacher and also quite capable of communicating dislike or disapproval. Peter Collingwood, Marianne Straub, Joyce Griffiths, Barbara Sawyer (whose subsequent teaching at Camberwell was to be such an important dissemination of Ethel Mairet's ideas), all came within her sphere of influence in one way or another. She wrote several short books on the part which handweaving had to play in contemporary society, including *Handweaving Today, Handweaving and Education*, and an excellent book on natural dyeing. She was elected a Royal Designer for Industry by the Royal Society of Arts.

Ethel Mairet was a great and far-reaching influence who presented hand-weaving as a living and creative element vitally contributive to contemporary education, to industry and to art. She was (though her appearance belied it) a real woman of her time – in an era erring towards cheap slickness, she knew just how much could be lost in terms of quality and good design, and sought to redress the balance.

Elizabeth Peacock (1880–1969)

When she was a young woman Elizabeth Peacock was taught to weave by Ethel Mairet, and for a short time they worked together in Sussex. In 1922 she set up her own weaving studio in a house on the Sussex downs, from where she was to operate until her death in 1969. She handspun yarns, particularly linen and wool, dyed them with natural dyes, and then proceeded to make cloth and objects which, like the work of her contemporary, the potter Bernard Leach, had utility, quality and artistry. Her best-known pieces of work are the hanging banners designed and woven for Dartington Hall in Devon, which depict the activities on the estate. They are truthful to the age in which they were made, well designed, beautifully proportioned and finely executed semi-abstracts. She experimented with draw-loom weaving, creating some beautiful, bold, geometric and abstract designs, and in 1951 she re-created exactly the textiles for Stone and Bronze Age figures in a display organized by the archaeologist, Jacquetta Hawkes for the prehistoric section of the South Bank Exhibition. She was a sound, gentle and quiet influence on her pupils and contemporaries. She taught at Reigate School of Art for 17 years and was a most considerate teacher. She also helped found the original Weavers, Spinners and Dyers Guilds. To Elizabeth Peacock, of utmost importance were the carding, spinning, dyeing and all the basic processes which lead to handweaving, playing a part, as they do, in the excellence of the final whole. Perhaps also one of her unique qualities was the fusion of good basic weaves with well-designed graphic concepts.

Other weavers

There were other weavers working at this time, perhaps not quite so well known. Alice Hindson specialized in designing for the draw-loom. Percy and Rita Beales, in Gloucestershire, spun and wove fine linen and wool and, like Elizabeth Peacock, made replica fabrics for the Jacquetta Hawkes Stone Age figures. Elsie Davenport was working both as a handweaver and teacher and wrote three excellent craft and technique orientated books on dyeing, spinning and weaving.

Pre-war weaving education

Sound technical weave teaching was in progress in various art schools. Walter Taylor, who had been a tapestry weaver apprentice at the William Morris Studios at Merton Abbey, set up a tapestry weaving department at the Central School of Arts and Crafts. The draw-loom and tapestry weaver, Luther Hooper, also taught at the Central and wrote several books on handweaving, notably *Hand-loom Weaving*. The Royal College of Art had a very small textile design department but students were sent to the Central School of Art to carry out practical work. The London School of Weaving, later incorporating the Kensington Weavers, was founded by Dorothy Wilkinson and operated mostly under her guidance between 1898 and 1970; painstaking technical instruction was to be obtained there also. In general terms, however, the study of handweaving in the schools encompassed limited aspects of the subject, with little aesthetic concern and a timid creative approach to yarns and colour. Dress or furnishing yardage, rug-weaving and tapestry weaving were the areas covered; everything was treated in a very flat and two-dimensional manner, sober in colour, confined in intent, and very much a craft as opposed to an art. Dress fabrics, in particular, rarely displayed any real feeling for fashion and were often almost indistinguishable from furnishing fabrics.

Post-1945 weaving education

It was not until well after the war that the British textile schools began to function with a vital creative force of their own. The City and Guilds of London Institute's examination on handweaving was instituted in the 1950s. It concentrated on techniques rather than design and came to an end in 1972; it has now been replaced by an all-embracing and far more realistic 'Fabric Structures' programme. The college-level diploma which could be undertaken was first, in 1935, called the Diploma in Industrial Design and then, after the war, the National Diploma in Design. It was, within limits, a worthwhile training and examined at national level. There were two woven textile syllabuses, one for handwoven dress and furnishing fabrics, the other for rug and tapestry weaving. Examination questions were safe, solid and fairly predictable. There was much emphasis on a sound, basic knowledge of materials and hand methods, but the Diploma course as a whole did not go far in real terms towards adequately training the student to design for industry or to become the complete artist-weaver. In fact at this time, in the art schools, there were wide divisions between the artists and the craftsmen.

Margaret Leischner

The Bauhaus textile influence in essence was disseminated strongly in Britain by Margaret Leischner, RDI; Bauhaus-trained in the school's earliest years, she became a member of staff there and later was appointed designer of furnishing fabrics at the Deutsche Werkstatten and the Berlin Modeschule der Stadt. In 1937 she was forced to seek safety in England where, ironically, she was interned during the war. Before and after the war she designed yarns and fabrics for many British textile firms, concentrating mainly on furnishings and floor coverings. Her fabrics were always true to Bauhaus tenets, using fibre, yarn and textile constructions in a truthful and absolutely contemporary way; she showed a total sensitivity to, and an understanding and mastery of the textile potential. The resulting fabrics were refreshing, honest and satisfying products on the British market, and they became the nation's pride in such showings as the 'Festival of Britain', the 'Britain Can Make It' Exhibition, and at the Design Centre when it was opened in 1956.

After the war the Royal College of Art in London was re-formed under the leadership of Sir Robin Darwin. Margaret Leischner was asked to head its textile department and her appointment in 1948 was to influence textile art training far beyond the confines of the college itself – in fact, most of the art schools in Britain where the textile discipline was seriously taught at National Diploma level. To quote Ruth Hurle, 'she built a system for the instruction of weaving which has become so absorbed into general practice as to have become almost anonymous' – a system based firmly on Bauhaus precepts. The Royal College of Art Weaving School, under Margaret Leischner, was, during this period, very much geared to designing for industry with the artist's eye. However, the Bauhaus tenets were so strongly underpinned with basic artistic practice, that the self-same teaching also laid the grounding that was to prove the foundations for the use of the textile medium to a fine-art end.

Towards the end of her 14-year period at the Royal College of Art, she was deeply involved in the formation of the new system which was to supersede the National Diploma in Design. The system was to be autonomous to each individual art college, and it could therefore vary from region to region. In 1961 the system became known as the Diploma in Art and Design (– a welcome addition of the word 'art'). In 1974, a number of courses were awarded the status of a Bachelor of Arts degree, some of which are second to none for sound and creative textile art training. A breath of contemporary air had been brought into the art colleges – a more realistic approach to designing for industry and a freer atmosphere for the development of the artist-weaver. In 1963, when speaking on the training of designers of woven textiles at the Queen Elizabeth College, she had said,

> I do not know how the Principals of Colleges of Art select the students who will study woven design. One gains the impression that students who want to study painting and are not quite up to it get passed on to textile design and those with no truly graphic ability get moved to woven design . . . Unhappily failed painters and graphic designers do not make designers of wovens. They are different breeds. The attitude of the art schools has been largely instrumental in hindering the development of woven design in this country. It is regarded largely as a craft . . .

Margaret Leischner was succeeded at the Royal College of Art in 1963 by Martin Hardingham as the head of the woven textile department. Students are all post-graduate and the textile school gives equal attention to hand and machine woven and knitted fabrics, to other forms of construction and methods such as laminating and bonding, and to the use of the textile medium to a purely expressionist end.

Marianne Straub

At the Royal College of Art for a period between 1970 and 1975, another equally great textile designer's influence was felt, that of Marianne Straub. Straub and Leischner were roughly contemporary with each other. While Margaret Leischner was at the RCA, Marianne Straub was in charge of wovens, first at the Central College of Art, then at Hornsey College of Art. They were both designing yarns and fabrics for the woven furnishing industry at roughly the same time. Both were deeply concerned with and active in the formation of new educative methods for textile designers.

Swiss-born Marianne Straub trained as a weaver at the Zurich School of Applied Arts, that training-ground of many great artists and designers, under Heinz Otto Hürlimann. Hürlimann was an early Bauhaus student and one of the finest handweavers in Europe. Marianne Straub came to England at the end of her Swiss training to study further in Bradford, after which she went to work in the studio of Ethel Mairet. From 1933 to 1936 she was employed by the Rural Industries Bureau to design for the Welsh woollen mills. In 1937 she joined Helios Ltd, a subsidiary firm of Barlow & Jones. In 1950 Warner & Sons Ltd took over the work that Helios were doing and Marianne Straub became an important member of Warner's design team with responsibility for contemporary, as opposed to the traditional, fabrics for which Warners had always been famous. She also became designer for Tamesa Fabrics (a position which she still holds), and between 1970 and 1975 she was a member of the staff at the RCA. Like Mairet and Leischner, her attitude to woven textiles is that of the artist. She approaches weaving with all the vision of the aesthetically creative mind, with total understanding of and respect for the raw materials which are her medium, and with a complete mastery of the technical means to design for twentieth-century production methods. Her fabrics are used in any scheme where the finest contemporary wovens are required, such as in aircraft, hotels, restaurants. In 1973 she too was elected Royal Designer for Industry, a precious accolade awarded by the Royal Society of Arts, London, and 1977 saw the publication of her book *Hand-Weaving and Cloth Design* (Pelham).

Designers like Leischner, Straub and Mairet were surely the final valid end-product of William Morris's ideology.

The influence of four people

Margaret Leischner and Marianne Straub were the great post-war influences mainly concerned with fabric yardage and yarn design, though their thinking is seminal to all textile construction. The two great influences in the textile fine-art area were Tadek Beutlich and Peter Collingwood. The work of these four people engendered a healthy and fruitful climate of creativity for those who were alive to it.

Beutlich and Collingwood, both of whose work is dealt with in detail in the main section of this book, emerged as Britain's two great artists in fibre in the 1960s and '70s. Beutlich was the first to enjoy the unheard-of privilege, in Britain, of having his work shown in galleries otherwise devoted to painting and sculpture. Peter Collingwood was accorded a similar honour in an exhibition with Hans Coper, the ceramist, at the Victoria and Albert Museum in 1969. The combined influence of these four weavers, all active from the '50s onward, and each an artist without peer in his or her own field, kept the general standard of serious textile work in Britain high.

Tadek Beutlich

Tadek Beutlich's influence was disseminated first-hand via his teaching at Camberwell School of Art between 1961 and 1974. Many of his tenets and attitudes come through in his book called *The Technique of Woven Tapestry*, published in 1967. It is a source of information, not only about technique (which is dealt with in a very lively and non-traditionalist manner) but also about attitudes and inspiration. His work was to be seen regularly at the Grabowski Gallery in 1963, 1967, 1969 and 1972 and in many major exhibitions, including 'Weaving for Walls' at the Victoria and Albert Museum in 1965, the Association of Guilds 'Woven Textiles '68' at the London Building Centre,

'Modern British Hangings' at the Scottish Arts Council Galleries, Edinburgh, in 1970, and the 'Craftsman's Art' exhibition at the Victoria and Albert Museum in 1973. He used fibre, thread, the woven construction and other materials in the manner of a sculptor and, as such, his work was a revelation indeed. In his work, for the first time in Britain, the textile medium was seen to be used absolutely and unequivocably to a fine-art end, and with total and utter relevance; for Beutlich's strength of vision no other medium would do.

Peter Collingwood

Peter Collingwood's work became known first through Heal's, the large furniture and interior design store in Tottenham Court Road, London. Heal's became practically the arbiters of taste on all contemporary interior design matters from the '30s onward. It was Heal's Craftsman's Market which first showed Collingwood's rugs. More gallery showings followed, his work was featured at the Design Centre in the Haymarket, and finally the Victoria and Albert Museum held a two-man exhibition, Coper–Collingwood, in 1969. Peter Collingwood was the first weaver ever to be accorded such attention in Britain. In 1974 he was awarded the Order of the British Empire. He is a great textile innovator. One essential quality of his work is that it is produced with the manufacturing time and effiency factor well in mind; it is therefore modestly priced, which means that a great many people can enjoy it at first hand. He is a researcher and scholar and also, fortunately, enjoys imparting his findings through his books, *Techniques of Rug Weaving* in 1967, *The Techniques of Sprang* in 1975, and *Tablet Weaving* yet to be published. His writings, mostly on technical matters, have also featured regularly in the *Journal* of the Association of Guilds of Weavers, Spinners and Dyers, in which he exhorts weavers to work with sincerity and to have a feeling for their time.

Other influences

During these formative years after the war, there were several other influences which played their part in creating a healthy atmosphere for the development of fine-art weaving. One of these was the firm of Hugh Griffiths, at first in Hull and then near Bath, who were suppliers of yarns to handweavers. Joyce Griffiths had worked with Ethel Mairet and therefore knew all about beautiful yarns in many varieties of construction and Hugh had been trained at the Royal College of Art in the 1930s and was a fine colourist. With the yarn sample cards sent out by the firm came tiny pieces of inventive and original woven designs made by Joyce Griffiths – her Mairet training much in evidence. These yarns and sample cards undoubtedly had enormous direct influence on weavers.

Another seemingly peripheral but in fact important influence was the loom-making firm of George and John Maxwell of Ditchling. These two, father and son, were craftsmen *par excellence*. They were not weavers themselves, but their looms were a joy to handle, and had within them the very essence of craftsmanship.

Book production was not, at that time, as prolific as it is now, but several books stand out as of enormous influence internationally. The book entitled *On Weaving*, written by Anni Albers, the artist-weaver, (previously a student at the Bauhaus) and wife of the painter Josef Albers, resident in the States, was not published until 1965, but it set out Bauhaus tenets and, where they concerned weaving, outlined textile materials and techniques as timeless methods and materials by which man could not only clothe himself but also make contemporary abstract statements. Two years earlier, in her evaluation of weaving for the *Encyclopaedia Britannica*, she had defined weaving as 'an art discipline able to convey understanding of the interaction between medium and process that results in form'. Tadek Beutlich's *Technique of Woven Tapestry* (1967) had a far broader approach to the subject than the title implies, and in the same year Peter Collingwood's *Techniques of Rug Weaving* was published, which has now become a standard work. An earlier book of great influence, published in 1955, small, modest, but of inestimable worth, was Mary Kirby's *Designing on the Loom*. Mary Kirby had trained at the Slade School of Art as a painter and at the Royal College of Art in textiles. She became a teacher of weaving at the Kingston and Central Schools of Art in Britain and at Kumasi School of Art in Ghana. She was a great traveller, textile researcher, scholar and a designer of wovens for industry. The fruits of all her skill and dedication went into the book which she illustrated with her own and her students' work. It was the first book which clearly delineated exactly how to use the loom creatively and how to design from first principles in a thoroughly professional manner. After her death the book was out of print for a long time but now it is available once more, its message as clear and valid now as it was when she wrote it.

The Association of Guilds of Weavers, Spinners and Dyers

Besides the designers, teachers, books, schools and courses of tuition after the war, there were several other influences which were to have a cumulative effect on the ultimate handweaving scene: the large textile firms, exhibitions, organizations and, of course, the guilds.

The original Guild of Weavers, Spinners and Dyers was formed in Dorset in 1930 and an exhibition of work was held at the Whitechapel Art Gallery in 1935. The Guilds functioned until the war in 1939 when, like many other institutions, they closed down. They were re-formed in 1950, flourished and grew in number, and the Association of Guilds was formed in 1956. The Guild journal, now called *Weavers Journal*, was started in 1952 and was, from the start, a source of excellent and impeccable information. A down-to-earth publication, its pages were and are full of informed writing by weavers like Ruth Hurle, Hilda Breed, Mary Barker, Margaret Seagrott, John Tovey, Theo Moorman, Ann Sutton, Peter Collingwood, and many more.

Unfortunately, the link between the guilds and the art colleges is not as strong and fruitful in Britain as it is in the USA. It seems to be caused by several things, the most significant perhaps being the different age groups prevalent in the two, but much benefit could be gained by both if closer co-operation could be achieved.

Warners and Morton Sundour

Two of the great textile firms which influenced the total textile scene were Warner & Sons Ltd and Morton Sundour Ltd. Warner & Sons Ltd of Braintree in Essex was originally a silk weaving firm of Spitalfields in the East End of London. An illustrious and honoured name in British machine and handwoven textiles, the company made damasks, brocades, and velvets of the finest quality possible, and its products have been the main source for Coronation robes, ceremonial regalia, and whenever the best was required. Alec Hunter, whose father was a handweaver of Jacquard fabrics, was the managing director during the firm's greatest years. A fine modern designer himself, Hunter was instrumental in starting the new department for the production of contemporary woven fabrics in which Theo Moorman worked from 1932 to 1939 and for which Marianne Straub became designer in 1950.

The second firm, Morton Sundour Ltd, one of the leading companies in the field of printed and woven textiles, fathered the Edinburgh Weavers Company, which was based in Carlisle. This new company was to allow Alastair Morton, the son of the firm's founder, to give full scope to his ideas, which were to bring all the inspiration of pure artists into textile mass-production, totally without compromise or dilution, by means of the creative freedoms now attained by designers on the handloom who were working for industry. The resulting fabrics were art works, sometimes the work of painters like Ben Nicholson and Mario Marini. Landscapes, figures, animal forms, geometric shapes and total abstracts were all translated into fabric, the like of which has probably never been seen since. Luxurious fibres, fancy yarn-spinnings, deep weave textures, were all part of the artistic whole, put together by Alastair Morton and his assistants. Of his method of working he said,

> The pure artists are the research workers of the world of art, the Newtons and Einsteins of art leading the way to discovery. . . . The technique which painters must master is the most subtle of any of the crafts, therefore they are the most free of any of the craftsmen to express their vision, they can range over the whole field of man's visual imagination. In the work of such men therefore there can be a wealth of colour, from composition and imagery. . . . A designer's mind must be open to all such fields of experience. . . .

Exhibitions

So, in the post-war period, the work of Leischner and Straub could be seen throughout Britain in interiors, quality textile stores, and exhibitions devoted to textile yardage. Beutlich's and Collingwood's work, on the other hand, was seen through exhibitions in art and craft galleries. Exhibitions played an immensely important part in the post-war textile scene. At first those in Britain were extremely modest, but as great works came into the country from Europe and the United States to be shown in London and sometimes to tour the provinces, gradually Britain's own exhibitions grew freer and stronger.

Beutlich, Sax Shaw, Archie Brennan and many others had been inspired by the exhibition of French Tapestries which came to the Victoria and Albert

Museum in 1948. It was to spark off a whole new way of approaching the art of tapestry. France was the mecca of tapestry weavers in the 1950s. For those Britons who travelled in other parts of Europe, there were revelations like the American Pavilion in the 13th Milan Triennale of 1964, showing, as it did, the shaped and pierced tapestry weaves of Lenore Tawney, 'King', 'Queen' and 'River'. There also was Dominic di Mare's three-dimensional weaving and Mary Walker Phillips' delicate knitted traceries. The Lausanne International Tapestry Biennales from 1962 onwards showed some of the finest textile art work in the world, and in Lausanne were the excellent one-man exhibitions by people like Jagoda Buic, Magdalena Abakanowicz, Sheila Hicks and Olga de Amaral.

In 1957 the Victoria and Albert Museum held 'The Crafts '57', organized by the Arts & Crafts Exhibition Society, where rugs and one or two tapestries and room-dividers showed the greatest merit. In 1962 the same museum caused to be brought to England a collection of works under the title 'Modern American Wallhangings' and here, for the first time (unless one had travelled in Europe) one could see the free, airy weaving of Lenore Tawney and Trude Guermonprez, the textured and colourful work of Alice Parrott, the perspex and linear room-dividers of Ted Hallman, and the work of many others who were using textile constructions, often in conjunction with manmade yarns and materials, to create weavings which were uninhibited by textile tradition and were direct art statements in fibre. The 'Woven Forms' exhibition of American-born but Paris-domiciled Sheila Hicks was another revelation, and was shown by Interiors International in 1963, who argued, after the 'Woven Forms' showing in New York of the work of Hicks, Tawney, Adams, Zachai and Zeisler, that it was imperative for Britain to see the best of what was being produced internationally. Here one was introduced, among other works, to small studies which seemed to be the essence of textile, like precious ancient fragments; one realized just how valid a fine art medium textile was, and how freely it should be used, without barriers erected between techniques – what did it matter whether Sheila Hicks was a weaver or an embroideress, as long as she was an artist?

The Association of Guilds held an exhibition called 'Weaving for Walls' at the Victoria and Albert Museum in 1965 which demonstrated clearly that British weavers were learning to meld their own sturdy and loom-based constructions with the freer and less loom-inhibited work from Eastern Europe and the USA. A more broadly-based and creative approach to weaving was being generated. 'Woven Textiles '68' followed at the London Building Centre. In both exhibitions, the work of Beutlich, Collingwood and Ann Sutton stood out above all others.

In 1966, the Grabowski Gallery brought to Britain the great fibre works and tapestries of Polish artists: Magdalena Abakanowicz, Wojciech Sadley, Zofia Butrymowicz and Jolanta Owidzka. The great fibre forms of Abakanowicz in particular were to place weave in the area of standing sculpture, and those of Sadley in the area of shaped and space hangings. The same gallery showed the crocheted forms of Ewa Jarosnyczka and exhibited Tadek Beutlich's work repeatedly. The British Crafts Centre showed the rugs and macrogauzes of Peter Collingwood in 1964 and 1973, the perspex and thread constructions, knitted forms, graphic images and furniture-like objects of Ann Sutton in 1969 and 1975, and the tapestry images of Edinburgh's Archie Brennan and the crocheted and woven sisal sculptures of Kathleen McFarlane in 1976, as well as group showings, generally of new, young artist-weavers. In 1972 the big, all-embracing exhibition 'Objects USA' was seen nationwide, and in 1974 the massive works of Abakanowicz, standing forms and heads, were shown in London at the White-chapel Art Gallery.

In 1970, during the Edinburgh International Festival of the Arts, the Scottish Arts Council mounted an exhibition in their galleries in Edinburgh called 'Modern British Hangings', which showed the work of 40 artists. This was a significant step, as the Edinburgh Festival usually confined its attention to the accepted arts of painting and sculpture. Work was varied in technique; the artificial barriers between differing textile constructions had fallen. 'Modern Hangings from Scotland', which followed closely afterwards, showed that the Scottish school itself was mainly concerned with the evolution of traditionally produced though by no means traditionally conceived tapestries, and work from the Edinburgh Tapestry Company and the tapestry school of Edinburgh College of Art figured prominently.

The Edinburgh Tapestry Company was founded in 1910 by the Marquis of . Bute, to produce traditional, figurative tapestries which were woven by master-weavers from William Morris's studios at Merton Abbey and later their Scottish apprentices. After the war, Ronald Cruickshank was the master-weaver and the work of British artists such as Graham Sutherland and Stanley Spencer was translated into small, domestic-scale tapestries.

In the 1950s, under new directorship, and under the artistic direction of Sax Shaw, it was lifted further into the mainstream of contemporary art thought. This was carried forward by Archie Brennan, who is artistic director of the company now. Under his guidance the studios have become unique and masterly in the production of original tapestries and in the ability of the staff to interpret drawn and painted tapestry designs in a free and creative manner on the loom. The School of Tapestry at Edinburgh College of Art also stemmed from Sax Shaw, its chief architect has been Archie Brennan, and it is now headed by Maureen Hodge. The 16-year retrospective exhibition of the work of its staff and students entitled 'Scottish Tapestry, loose ends, close ties and other struc-tures' in 1977 demonstrated its strength and continuing sense of purpose. Here true tapestry is seen in its most contemporary and vital form and at its most dedicately produced level. The stream of artists, Maureen Hodge, Fiona Mathison, Fionna Geddes, to name but three, who are the product of the school or who have been deeply influenced by it, is steady and constant.

It was in Edinburgh, and partly as a result of the 1970 Scottish Arts Council Exhibition and its attendant seminars, that 'Weavers Workshop' was conceived. It was a brave effort and in its short life there were some fine exhibitions of textile art mounted but it was beaten by the raw economic winds that were to blow across Britain in the mid 1970s. Partly as a result of 'Modern British Hangings', came the Camden Arts Centre's 'Experimental Textiles' show in 1971, organized by Martin Hardingham, Head of Woven Textiles at the Royal College of Art. A year later, at the same centre, 'Woven Structures' was mounted by the Crafts Advisory Committee. In both these exhibitions British work at its best was exhibited together with work by international artists. Meanwhile, the Lausanne Tapestry Biennales continue every two years to show some of the finest work being produced internationally. However, work shown at Lausanne has to be not less than 5 sq m (16 sq ft) in area, which excludes the work of vast numbers of serious artists. In 1974 at the British Crafts Centre in London, in an effort to fill part of the void, the International Exhibition of Miniature Textiles was conceived and inaugurated. This has been the catalyst which has highlighted a whole new method of working to many artists.

The British Crafts Centre is a membership organization, but it receives considerable financial and moral support from the government-sponsored Crafts Advisory Committee, which was set up in 1971 to aid and encourage artists and craftsmen. This was the first time such positive and direct government help had ever been forthcoming in the sphere of woven art, and was an immense step forward. The CAC's first big exhibition was 'The Craftsman's Art' at the Victoria and Albert Museum in 1973 in which the work of, among others, Collingwood, Beutlich, Sutton, McFarlane, Brennan, Cox, Gilby, Hodge, Riegler and Sönju was seen. The CAC publish an excellent magazine called *Crafts*. *Crafts* and *Weavers Journal* are the main and almost only regular disseminations of information about textile art in Britain, as other art magazines still pay the movement little heed.

The British Crafts Centre's International Exhibition of Miniature Textiles was an effort to fill part of the void left by the size regulations of the Lausanne Biennales. The next logical step could be, not to inaugurate yet a third category with its own venue, but to realize size for what it is – irrelevant to the merit of the work. The final step of all, of course, can only be when the works are no longer exhibited in special showings, linked to techniques and materials, but integrated totally into the art world and shown in galleries alongside painting and sculpture where the finest of them undoubtedly belong.

Conclusions

This chapter has traced, in broad terms, the major developments of handweaving in Britain over the past years which have had some bearing on the particular aspect of the subject dealt with in this book. The watershed seemed to be the war period of 1939–45, after which nothing was quite the same. Bauhaus-based thinking had gathered momentum, and the handloom and textile materials were seen as valid vehicles not only for intelligent design for industry, but also for the realization of abstract thought. Having achieved this breakthrough, it was only a matter of time before not only weavers themselves but also others seeking a fluent vehicle for their creative wills would come to use the loom and textile materials and techniques as their chosen medium.

Those artists whose work is illustrated in the following pages have started from all points of the compass: some were weavers, some painters, some graphic artists, and so on. It is a matter of some interest to make note of the manner in which individuals have developed and the paths each has taken. Peter Collingwood, once he had forsaken medicine, firmly architected his own weave training, seeking out the finest minds with whom to work, like those of Ethel Mairet and Alastair Morton. Theo Moorman, though weave-trained, felt her particular style of training to be inadequate for the result she sought to achieve. She gained the collaboration of a sculptor to help her orientate her work towards being a vehicle for her semi-abstract visual concepts rather than towards the production of cloth, for which she had been trained. Robert Mabon began as an interior designer, but taught himself to weave, and finally surrendered himself to the delights of both weave and ceramics; he enjoys both these media equally, and some of his finest work is produced when he melds the two. Kathleen McFarlane began life as a librarian and translator until a continuing sense of personal unfulfilment led her to paint. Meanwhile she had been taught to weave in Norway in order to produce domestic textile goods. It was when she realized, by seeing the work of Abakanowicz, that the loom could also be the tool of the artist, that everything fell into place for her. Bobbie Cox began as a painter and art teacher, but when travel caused her to come into contact with people who were using fibre-spinning, dyeing and weaving, she saw in these materials and methods first a sensitive medium for the teaching situation, and then the perfect means by which to transmit her own visual preoccupations. Alec Pearson had been an art teacher, lecturer and water-colourist for most of his life, but a few years ago he realized that tapestry and wool had unique qualities which transmitted certain facets of his feelings about the lakes and mountains of Cumbria better than any other. Fionna Geddes studied drawing and painting, but proximity to the tapestry school at Edinburgh College of Art caused her to do a postgraduate course in textiles, and now in her mixed media works textile is both the medium and the message. Maureen Hodge, by contrast, has been a tapestry weaver almost from the start, so has Archie Brennan; Ann Sutton was also textile trained. Sax Shaw, like Robert Mabon, has equal love for more than one material, being equally skilful in and dedicated to both stained glass and tapestry; he also works in metal.

The work of both Peter Collingwood and Ann Sutton is cool and mathematically logical, they are both textile innovators and forward-thinkers – breakers of new ground. Archie Brennan, Unn Sönju, and Fiona Mathison are all concerned with very graphic imagery through the medium of tapestry. The work of Fionna Geddes has something in common with that of the Colombian, Olga de Amaral, and the American, Sheila Hicks, seeming to be about the essence of textile itself. Alec Pearson and Sax Shaw both use traditional flat tapestry to give substance to visions that are very much those of the painter. Theo Moorman's work is quiet, subtle, gentle, Myriam Gilby's full of movement and vigour, but both are concerned with three-dimensionalizing. Some artists are inspired by the very sources or concepts which switch others off. A particular way of working may be a boon to one and anathema to another.

Everyone's path to the same point is by a different route. The point at which they all aim is the absolute realization of each unique vision. Thus highly motivated, artists are restless, and search until the perfect medium for their particular vision is found which will transmit their ideas with the utmost fluidity and the least compromise and through which they can find themselves still further. Such media are those of the loom and textile techniques, now that they are emancipated from traditionalist restraints and internationally recognized as valid fine-art media. The result has produced some of the strongest art statements of the mid twentieth century.

The Work of 17 British Artist-weavers

Tadek Beutlich

ALICANTE, SPAIN

Tadek Beutlich was born in Lwowek, Poland, in 1922. He studied art in Poland, Germany and Italy, his ambition being to become a painter.

In 1947 he came to England and attended the Sir John Cass School of Art in London for a year. It was in London that he saw the exhibition of French tapestries at the Victoria and Albert Museum and this was an important step for him. He watched the French tapestry craftsmen weaving at the exhibition and decided he wanted to weave tapestries himself, so he made a small frame on which he produced his first effort. As weaving was not taught at the Sir John Cass School, he moved to Camberwell School of Art where he studied weaving under Mrs J. Drew and Barbara Sawyer. However, the training at Camberwell did not then cover tapestry weaving in any detail, and so he was obliged to teach himself the technique.

From 1951 to 1974 he was a visiting lecturer at the Camberwell School of Art and it was early in this period that his influence on weaving in Britain was first felt. It was, in any case, a time of rethinking among textile artists, and it was Beutlich and Collingwood who demonstrated most forcibly the new-found freedom from the restrictions which the loom, approached in a certain way, can impose.

In 1967 he moved into 'Gospels' in Sussex, once the studio of that earlier great weaver, thinker and writer, Ethel Mairet; having now two large studios at his disposal, he could weave larger-sized hangings, and his work began to take on a monumental quality. In 1967 Beutlich wrote *The Technique of Woven Tapestry*, in which he demonstrated clearly the validity of fibre and yarn and the woven technique as an art medium, often illustrating his points by his own early work. In a review of the book I commented that his works are 'intimations of immor-

1.1

1.3

1.2

1.1 *View of Tadek Beutlich's studio from his house*

1.2 *Tadek Beutlich and* Archangel

1.3 Bird of Prey *(1972), 180cm × 270cm (6ft × 9ft); black mohair warp; sisal weft*

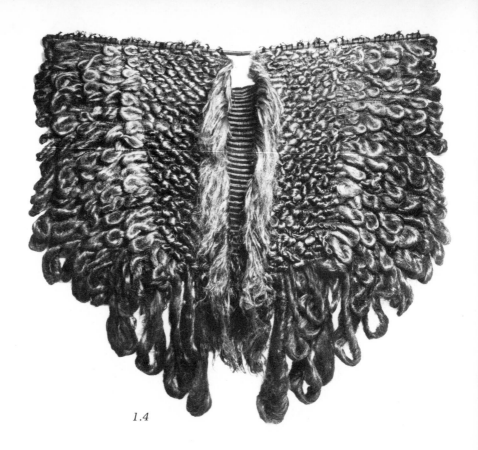

1.4

tality', which indeed they are. They have changed in style and technique over the years. His first tapestries showed a delicacy of handling and materials, with the accent on fine thread and flat weaving whether he was working in tapestry technique using cotton twine warps at 8 ends per 2·5 cm (1 inch), combining tapestry with plain weave, using double cloth techniques, or using the sparse open technique seen in illustration 1.5. His later works moved towards a monumentality in scale and concept when they became more and more three-dimensional (illustrations 1.3, 1.4). His present work shows an absorption with the intimate and the miniature (illustrations 1.6, 1.7, 1.8, 1.9, 1.12, 1.14). Always the underlying theme seems to be about the eternal, and he uses moon, sun, landscape, insect and bird forms as the vehicle. Large works are often seamed to achieve areas of concavity, which add emphasis to the massive twists of heavy, unspun sisal and jute, thus allowing the characteristics of the material to come into their own, something which is always Beutlich's main concern. Since 1963 he has exhibited regularly in British and international galleries and his hangings are illustrated in all major works on fibre-art.

In 1973 he moved from England to Spain where he now lives and works. In 1974 and 1976 he was invited by the British Crafts Centre to participate at the International Exhibition of Miniature Textiles. The problem of producing something not larger than 20cm in any direction absorbed him greatly, giving him ideas for a more intimate and closely observed type of work. One result of living in Spain is now the addition to the materials which he uses of esparto grass and stone-like shapes of processed cotton wool. But his preoccupations are still with the same themes (illustrations 1.10, 1.11, 1.12, 1.13, 1.15, 1.16) and particularly that of the moon.

1.4 Eruption *(1970), 280cm × 325cm (9ft 4in × 10ft 10in); black mohair warp; black mohair, unspun jute and dyed sisal weft*

1.5 Triptych *(1968), 220cm × 300cm (7ft 6in × 10ft); fine linen warp; linen, jute, wool, bark and X-ray film weft*

24

1.5

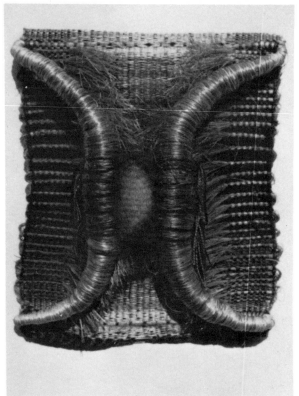

1.6

1.7

1.8

1.9

1.6 Dawn *(1974), 20cm × 20cm (10in × 10in); sisal and jute*

1.7 Little Moon *(1974), 20cm × 20cm × 4cm (10in × 10in × 2in); cotton warp; paper, wood, jute and sisal weft*

1.8 Little Moon *(1974) 20cm × 20cm (10in × 10in); sisal and jute*

1.9 Sunset *(1974), 20cm × 20cm × 3cm (10in × 10in × 1in); sisal and jute*

1.10 Reflection of the Moon *(1977), 91cm × 120cm (3ft × 4ft); nylon warp; esparto, sisal, jute and processed cotton-wool weft*

1.11

1.12

1.13

1.14

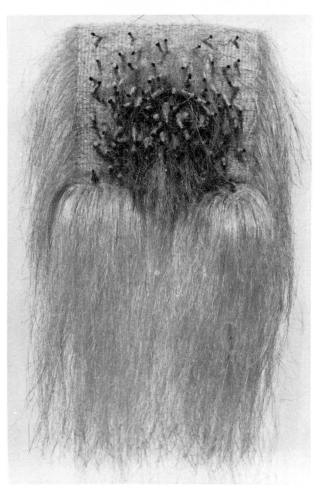

1.16

1.15

1.11 Four Phases of the Moon *(1977),*
91cm × 270cm (3ft × 9ft); nylon warp;
esparto, sisal and processed cotton-wool
weft

1.12 Fungi II *(1976), 20cm × 20cm (10in ×*
10in); nylon warp; wool, esparto, sisal,
jute and processed cotton-wool weft

1.13 Nature Study *(1977), 91cm × 120cm*
(3ft × 4ft); nylon warp; esparto, sisal,
jute and processed cotton-wool weft

1.14 Red, Orange and Yellow *(1976),*
18cm × 18cm × 13cm (9in × 9in × 5in);
nylon warp; wool, esparto, sisal, jute
and processed cotton-wool weft

1.15 Moonworshipper I *(1973), 127cm ×*
203cm (4ft 2in × 6ft 8in); sisal and jute

1.16 Germination *(1977), 60cm × 110cm*
(2ft × 3ft 8in); nylon warp; sisal and
wool weft

29

Archie Brennan

EDINBURGH

Archie Brennan was born near Edinburgh in 1931, and his father was an engineer. A strong talent for drawing manifested itself in his early years, and while still at school he attended life-drawing classes in the evenings. It was at these classes, at the local art school, that he met apprentice weavers from the Edinburgh Tapestry Company. When he was sixteen, he joined the company and worked there for five years as one of the team of apprentice tapestry-weavers working on sketches, paintings and cartoons by various British artists. The training and the work was orthodox, classical, traditional and thorough, and it was the latter quality which particularly appealed to one side of Brennan's complex character.

In 1952 the company's master-weaver, Ronald Cruickshank, set up his own workshop, the Golden Targe, and Archie Brennan joined him, working with him for two years until the studio was moved to America. Instead of going to America, he took himself to France, that mecca of tapestry weavers in the 1950s, for two years in order to draw, paint and study the design and production of tapestry. Of this decision he says, 'It had been intense at the workshops, yet isolated, I needed to look abroad to seek other arguments, other attitudes. France was the obvious place and a period there, whilst not providing many answers, raised and crystallized a number of questions.' Meeting Pierre Baudouin, that great cartonnier promoter and enthusiast, and Pierre Pauli, the mind behind the Lausanne Tapestry Biennales, was immensely important to him. Their fresh and open views led Brennan to formulate a conclusion that is with him still – that 'there is no "right" way in tapestry. There are no finite rules, systems or attitudes. Each of us moves through our experience, our examination of work from the past and that of our contemporaries

2.1

and settle for our own values and priorities as long as we hold them.'

National Service then ordained a two-year period when he was stationed in Carlisle, and there he managed to continue studying, this time concentrating on life-drawing and printed textiles. This break in his career led him to the conclusion that it was time to undertake a full-time art course and this he did at the Edinburgh College of Art, studying painting and stained glass in Sax Shaw's department. Such was Shaw's dual love of glass and tapestry, that Brennan was able to pursue his tapestry involvement in this ambience and was, in fact, awarded Edinburgh's first Diploma in Tapestry via the stained-glass department. He followed up this success with an Andrew Grant post-graduate scholarship with which he studied tapestry exclusively.

During 1962, a crucial year for him, he was appointed by the College to set up a

separate tapestry department, and returned to work at the Edinburgh Tapestry Company becoming within the year the Weaving Director – and all this in addition to his own work. Of this period he says,

> I was already prepared to set up as a solo tapestry weaver but these two opportunities offered other possibilities. I had no great ambition to be a successful artist-weaver but did want to help further establish tapestry as a worthwhile, if minor, medium. I wanted to see in Edinburgh, because I was there, a healthy thriving situation where experience, facilities, materials, equipment and enthusiasm was on a large scale. The established workshop had the basis, the new department the possibility.

Thus he took on his triple role, that of Weaving Director of the Tapestry Company (a post which combined the duties of Master Weaver and Designer, the latter post being previously held by Sax Shaw), Head of the new Tapestry School at the College of Art, and artist-weaver – a formidable burden of interlinked responsibilities; yet to each facet he gave his undiluted attention. To this role he set a time limit of ten years. Those ten years were to be fruitful ones indeed, for all three concerns. He has prodigious energy and vigour, enormous dedication and sense of responsibility to the tapestry art, and enthusiasm and involvement with work in hand, be it his own, another artist's, a fellow-weaver's or a student's. Along with these qualities and perhaps almost because of their very intensity, he exhibits a

2.1 *Archie Brennan*

2.2 *Archie Brennan and* Kitchen Range *(1973), 100cm × 120cm (39in × 48in); wool tapestry, woven by Edinburgh Tapestry Company (property of Michael Laird, ARIBA)*

31

2.3

2.3 Dark Island *(k.2.tog) (1971), 160cm ×*
100cm (67in × 39in); mixed tapestry
techniques including soumak, horsehair
weft; woven by Archie Brennan
(property of Victoria and Albert Museum,
London)

32

slightly ambivalent attitude towards working in the medium of tapestry. Many of his graphic images are quirky, as if to ridicule his very dedication to the medium by using off-beat images and *trompe-l'oeil* visual effects which can both amuse and irritate the observer while proclaiming in every fibre his supreme and absolute mastery of the tapestry technique.

One of his major contributions to the tapestry art when in his capacity as Director of the Company is that of being the catalyst between the weaver and the artist, if they are not one and the same person. The Company is without peer in the ability of its staff to interpret a painted or drawn cartoon in lively and honest textile terms. Brennan redesigned looms, widened the range of materials used, and re-examined weaving methods; of his most important contribution, he says,

> We sought, with a growing team, to find a particular approach to each work, thus bringing about a wider range of skills and a more open attitude. I held back and tried to understand what was particular in each work and how it could be realized into a tapestry which would have a life of its own.

In his own work, whether produced by himself in his studio at home, or by the weavers at the Tapestry Company, his contribution is in the field of the translation of the graphic image into flat tapestry. His 'switch-ons' are the bric-à-brac of contemporary life, television images, sport, clothes thrown down, cards, games, parcels, tyre treads, postcards, food wrappers, what he calls 'contemporary archaeology', but, above all, with textile itself, pattern, folds, the pattern of textile. Revel Oddy described Archie Brennan's family-taboo studio as 'an enlarged and more varied version of a woman's handbag'.

As a teacher and mentor he has been the chief architect of a vital, flourishing and unique tapestry school in Edinburgh. 'I knew that in the school I had to reduce technical training to a matter of weeks instead of years. I wanted a creative approach, more "what" and "why" rather than "how". With classical tapestry weaving as a basis students explored all manner of variations. They became in touch with what was going on around the world and

2.4

readily responded.' The students were expected to be as single-minded to the tapestry cause as he was, and committed to unremitting hard work for three years, both in weave-technique and in drawing. The standard of their work has consistently proved the strength and power of his teaching and precepts. This is not to indicate that they are recognizable as products of Edinburgh, except in their skills and attitudes. Each student is treated as totally individual and each confrontation is a personal tutorial: 'A student should finish with a growing understanding of himself or herself; an appetite for involvement and a thirst to look, see, examine, question and try to answer.'

Since 1964 there was a regular passing through the Tapestry Company workshops of the Art College graduates. The contribution they made, the contrast to the more professional experience of the workshop-

2.4 *Tapestry in whites and naturals (1970),*
330cm × 540cm (132in × 216in); woven
by the Edinburgh Tapestry Company
(commissioned by the Scottish Arts
Council for the Committee Room,
Charlotte Square, Edinburgh)

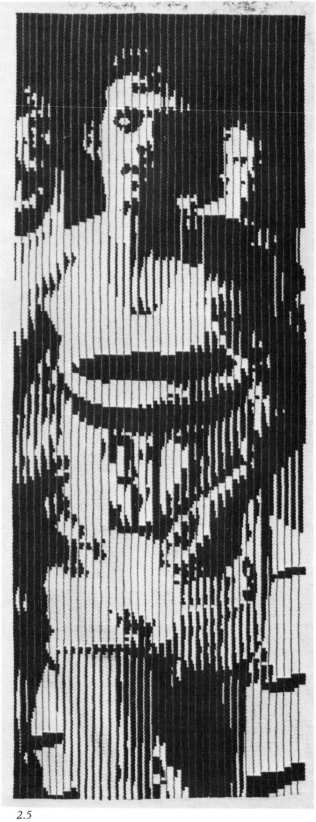

2.5

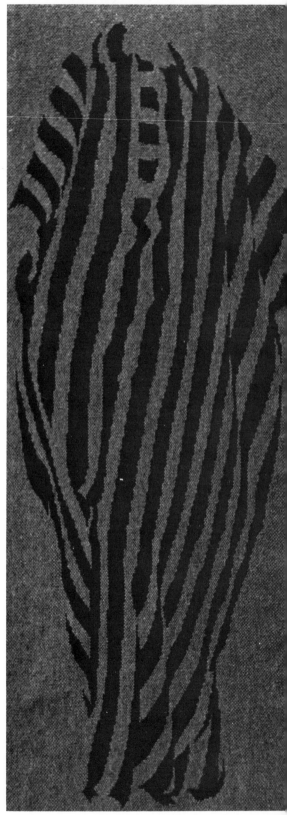

2.6

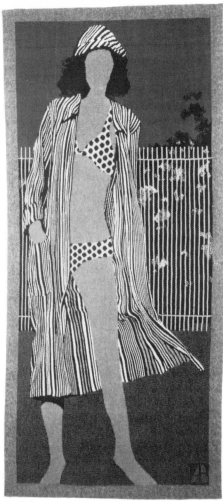

2.7

2.8

trained staff, what they gained from working in a practical setting and what they gave by their open, less orthodox approaches was invaluable to both workshop and school.

Archie Brennan's three-fold career – a massive undertaking for anyone – came to an end in 1973 when he elected to hand over his commitments at the College to his first student, Maureen Hodge, who was by now a considerable force entirely in her own right. Essentially the change was to allow him to concentrate more on the production and development of his own work. In 1974 he was awarded the Scottish Arts Council's first major Art Prize. Brennan finds teaching an enriching experience – so his teaching commitments merely changed to encompass a broader field than Edinburgh alone. He is now

visiting lecturer and consultant in various colleges in the UK and abroad, in countries as far distant as Australia and New Guinea.

2.5 Runner *(1976), 200cm × 81cm (80in × 33in); black and white wool tapestry, woven by Archie Brennan (property of the National Gallery of Victoria, Melbourne, Australia)*

2.6 For the Autumn of '75 *(1976), 200cm × 75cm (80in × 30in); tapestry, woven by Archie Brennan*

2.7 For the Summer of '75 *(1976), 190cm × 89cm (76in × 35in); tapestry, woven by Archie Brennan*

2.8 At a Window IV *(1976), 120cm × 86cm (48in × 34in); tapestry, woven by Archie Brennan (property of Dr Renate Schostack, Frankfurt, Germany)*

35

2.9

2.10

He says of his own tapestry work,

The process of looking, seeing, questioning, selecting and rejecting is the basis
of all the work I carry out. I draw in
order to learn to look, to see. I draw
and photograph to examine, to analyse
and to wonder. In the course of time my
work has narrowed down and I have
settled to work in a manner not far from
traditional tapestry, producing work that
is graphic rather than structural or
sensual; flat and orthodox rather than
sculptural or organic. There are a
number of themes that run consistently
through my work. . . . I seek to establish
and pinpoint the extraordinary qualities
of the most everyday things in our time.
I find so much in everyday living, in the
commonplace, that I cannot envisage
moving far from this. I work graphically,
using drawing, photography or 'ready-
made' imagery because I hold a belief
that, at best, the world outside should
find its way into tapestry as a language
to be learned, but above all to *use* and to
further develop the language only when
the work in question requires such.
Much I have done is to do with illusion,
particularly that of cloth and fabric. At
least by weaving, the cloth is halfway
to being real. From this I have moved on

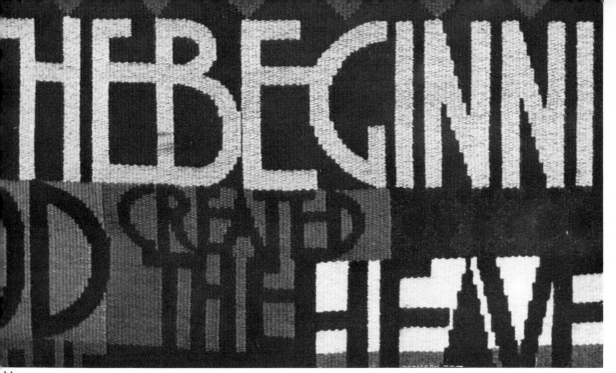

11

to the juxtaposing of cloth and 'impossible' materials, wood, paper, paint, print and photography. I have a constant fascination with making permanent the ephemeral nature of news and newsprint and with the camera – not only because photography freezes action and time but that it can record, as in moving water, or in sport, things that the human eye cannot see. Humour, wit and whimsy regularly occur in my work. I suspect, but don't wish to examine too closely, that this is a reaction to the long days and weeks required to produce a work that is non-utility, even useless, a pretend throwaway attitude so that, when the joke is over, there is underlying another structure and form that is the real basis of the tapestry. In a period where the sensual, tactile nature of the textile art has predominated with much justification and purpose, I have rarely worked heavily towards this; partly because I fear my ability to control such seductive characteristics, but perhaps because it is not a suitable vehicle for my interests. I use, as necessary, surface quality, alternative textile processes, three-dimensions, colour, etc., but always subjected to the needs, as I see them, of the aims, the end results. If there is one aspect of the process that I indulge in, it is in the

restriction – and scope – of the order of weaving. That it grows from one edge or one point, onwards; that the weaver completes a passage and moves on. Never to be able to radically change yesterday's or last week's work. This is an aspect of weaving that has little in common with painting and more in common with music and, indeed, living. In perspective, I find myself as a maker of tapestries at a time when Western society permits, if only just, a person to indulge in what is largely seen as a preoccupation with the making of 'useless' objects. As a craftsman, far removed from the earlier times when such had a readily recognized part to play in the social scheme, I am pleased to occupy my days with such indulgence.

2.9 Portraits *(1971), 200cm × 315cm (6ft 6in × 10ft 6in); tapestry, woven by Edinburgh Tapestry Company (property of Lady Stair's House, Edinburgh)*

2.10 *Two Tapestries for the Sanctuary Wall of St Cuthbert's Roman Catholic Church, Edinburgh (1971), each 426cm × 101cm (14ft × 3ft 4in); woven by Edinburgh Tapestry Company*

2.11 *Detail of St Cuthbert's Church Tapestries*

37

Geraldine Brock

NOTTINGHAMSHIRE

Geraldine Brock was born in Liverpool in 1938. She attended Liverpool College of Art and Design between 1955 and 1959 studying for the Diploma in Art and Design, Printed Textiles. As she concluded her Diploma Course she was awarded a Royal Society of Arts (London) travelling scholarship for textile design and with this she travelled extensively in Europe.

She then began her career as a freelance printed textile designer, producing at the same time a range of batik and tie-dye silks for craft centres throughout Britain. She had done a little weaving as an adjunct to the printed textiles course while she was still a student but it was the exhibition of Finnish rya rugs at the Victoria and Albert Museum, London, in 1960 which revealed to her the wider scope that weaving might have for her. She bought one of the rugs, a deep blue and black abstract by Kirsti Invesalo, together with an 86cm (34in) wide upright two-shaft loom, and began weaving.

Her earliest work explored the rya technique, using many hundreds of her own dyed colours in fine worsted yarn to create vibrant colour, tone and texture. The rya technique is one in which a knotted pile is inserted into a woven ground. The ground can vary in density. The pile can be closely or sparsely inserted, knotted singly or in groups. Mixtures of varied yarns can be used together in one knot, thus creating a deep, rich colour. The overriding characteristic of rya, however, is that the pile is a long shaggy one. Thus it is an excellent technique for the display of yarn type and variation, colour, lustre and texture. The pile drops vertically, or falls about depending on whether the rya object is laid flat or hung vertically.

From this first interest in rya, Geraldine Brock moved on to exploration in flat tapestry. A large commission for Liverpool University gave her the opportunity to

3.1

develop this interest in flat tapestry, as opposed to rya knotting, on a large scale. In this 420cm × 210cm (16ft × 8ft) tapestry (illustration 3.6), the design was to some extent governed by the width of her loom. The final piece was in five unequal strips seamed together and hung horizontally. This required the careful consideration of the joins as part of the entire design. The final cohesion of the whole is masterly.

A number of pieces followed using a combination of knotting and tapestry, with netting twine used for the warp, set at 4–6 ends per 2.5cm (1in). The tapestry served as a framework for surface decoration in the form of various knotting techniques, plaiting, twisting, binding, knitted and crochet strips, hanking, etc. (illustration 3.2). Through a greater understanding of these varied, simple techniques, she felt she was beginning to develop a

3.1 *Geraldine Brock*

3.2 Award Yourself the CDM *(1969),*
150cm × 80cm (5ft × 2ft 8in); tapestry
woven with knots and cut and uncut pile;
white and natural in pile, brightly
coloured tapestry stripes

38

3.3

3.4

more personal approach towards the content of her work, weaving pieces which were pastiches of traditional forms.

A passionate admiration for Turkish and nomadic rugs led to the use of the prayer rug form as inspiration for a series of hangings (illustration 3.3) which continues through to her present uncompleted piece, *Prayer Square* (illustration 3.4). This has a white field with a three-dimensional tapestry woven pile leading through to a ground of stripes and triangles in very rich, deep colour (illustration 3.5). The acquisition of a wider loom has removed some of her design problems.

The preparatory designs are very carefully worked out cartoons (see illustration 3.4) but with room still for creative work on the loom. The handling of yarns and the selection of colour is strong and instinctive. She dyes all her own yarns, mainly with chemical dyes and occasionally with natural dyes; *Prayer in an Eastern Garden* uses a combination of both.

From 1963 to 1968 she was colour and design consultant to Lancaster Carpet Co. in Manchester and from 1966 for ten years she was lecturer in the School of Fashion and Textiles at Liverpool Polytechnic. In 1976 she and her architect husband moved from the north-west to the Nottingham area, and she is now visiting lecturer in tapestry at Trent Polytechnic.

She says, 'I prefer to rely on design, colour, weft effects rather than "structure".' What seems particularly rare and unique in her work is her ability to fuse indissolubly, in one piece, traditional flat tapestry technique with the free and uninhibited use of fibre and yarn, two methods of working which, more often than not, appeal to different adherents.

3.3 *Detail of* Prayer in an Eastern Garden *(1973), 150cm × 165cm (5ft × 5ft 6in); tapestry woven with knotted pile (property of the Department of the Environment)*

3.4 *Cartoon for* Prayer Square *(1976), 210cm × 210cm (8ft × 8ft)*

3.5 *Weaving detail of* Prayer Square

3.6 *Tapestry hanging (1966), 420cm × 210cm (16ft × 8ft) (commissioned by Liverpool University for the Lecture Theatre)*

3.5

3.6

Peter Collingwood, O.B.E.

NAYLAND, SUFFOLK

Peter Collingwood was born in London in 1922. His father was a Professor of Physiology, and he studied medicine at St Mary's Hospital, London, and qualified as a doctor himself in 1946. He spent his two years' compulsory army service as a doctor stationed in England and then volunteered to serve with the Red Cross in Jordan. He had always, as a child, been interested in constructing things and it was in Jordan that he became intrigued with the technical process of weaving, by observing the work of local weavers. He had made himself a portable loom when working as a house surgeon immediately after qualifying and, influenced by the words of Eric Gill, 'the thing you like doing should be your work', he rethought his profession and, in 1950, left his medical career to become a weaver. Yet the scientific training he had undergone left him with a way of working which is fundamental to his success.

He took himself to the best of teachers, first to that pioneer educator and handweaver, Ethel Mairet, in her workshop at Ditchling in Sussex. Under her critical tutelage he lived and breathed a total sensitivity to colour, texture and innovative yarn and weave constructions. After working with Mairet, Collingwood moved on to the London studio of Birmingham-born Barbara Sawyer, who had also come under the influence of Mairet. This time he wanted to gain particular experience in the designing and weaving of rugs.

Finally he went to the studios of another great pioneer of design, Alastair Morton of Carlisle, whose 'Edinburgh Weaver' range of furnishing fabrics (for which well-known artists like Ben Nicholson were often commissioned to design) were, in the post-way years, such a joy and a delight in their application of artistry to the product of the power-loom.

Peter Collingwood's self-motivated tex-tile training came, therefore, direct from some of the finest and most creative minds there were.

While working with Alastair Morton, Collingwood had been perfecting his rug-weaving techniques and, in 1952, having decided that rugs were the most viable form of handweaving by which to earn a living, he established his own workshop at Highgate in London and set about the arduous business of weaving and selling hand-woven rugs, working very much from a 'cost and output' basis. Many of the rugs went to Heal's of Tottenham Court Road, who organized his first exhibition.

In 1958 Collingwood was invited to take up residence at Digswell House Arts Centre at Welwyn Garden City in Hertfordshire, a large country house with many outbuildings which had been adapted to accommodate craftsmen. Here he established contact with architects who found in his work elements which complemented their contemporary interiors: work which had moved on from rugs alone to airy, linear wallhangings. At this point also, he became involved with the Design Centre in the Haymarket, London, where his work was and still is frequently exhibited. It was he who was chosen to create the 'splendid woollen' stair-hanging which was presented to the Director, Sir Gordon Russell, on his retirement in 1959. In 1963 he was awarded a gold medal for his *Anglefell* textile (illustration 4.4) at the International Handcrafts Exhibition in Munich.

In 1964 Peter Collingwood, now married, moved his family to what is their present home, a school-house in the Suffolk village of Nayland near Colchester, set in a flat, misty, open landscape. The move was not because of any particular love of the

4.1 *Peter Collingwood and a macrogauze*

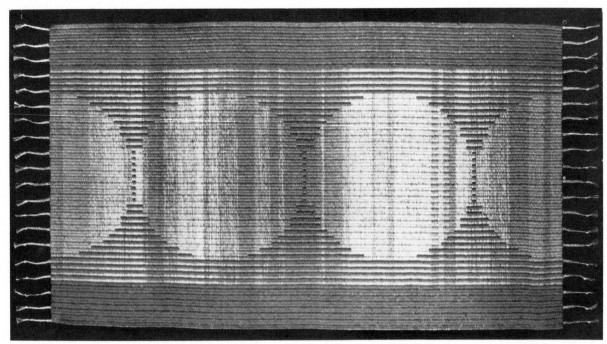

4.2

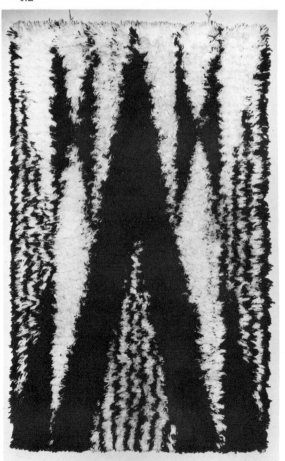

4.3

4.4

44

country but because the red-brick Victorian school-buildings provide excellent, practical, lofty working-space. In the workshop there are five large looms with all the attendant apparatus. The looms have been skilfully restructured by Peter Collingwood himself to his own particular purposes. It is the loom's precision and control which is its fascination for him – he calls some of his work 'a kind of thread engineering'. In no one's hands has the loom become more flexible, malleable and 'biddable' as a design tool. His loom techniques are mainly three-fold, 'corduroy' weave for pile rugs (illustration 4.3), 'shaft-switching' for flat rugs (illustration 4.2) for which the basic loom-mechanism is added to, and 'macrogauze' for linear wallhangings (illustrations 4.6, 4.7, 4.9) for which the loom is stripped of some of its working parts.

The 'corduroy' rug technique is achieved by so threading the warp that when the weft is thrown, it interlaces with the warp for 5cm (2in) and then floats over the next 5cm (2in) and so on across the full width. The floats are then cut in their centres to make the pile.

The 'shaft-switching' technique for flat rugs is achieved by a lever system above the four shafts which enables the threading of the warp to be altered *during* weaving. By this means two-colour patterns can be quickly and simply woven, which would otherwise require a Jacquard loom.

Finally, the 'macrogauze' technique for wallhangings, in which the usually immovable and sternly parallel warp threads move from one place in the piece to another, is achieved by threading the warp into sections of rigid heddle 2.5cm (1in) wide, housed in a special batten which can rise and fall and so give the two necessary sheds. Each of these miniature warps is wound on a separately weighted bobbin so, no matter what oblique course

4.2 *Rug, with wool weft, using shaft-switching technique*

4.3 *Pile rug; corduroy technique in wool*

4.4 *Anglefell 5, 90cm × 180cm (3ft × 6ft); natural linen*

4.5 *Three-dimensional Macrogauze 5; white linen, stainless steel rod*

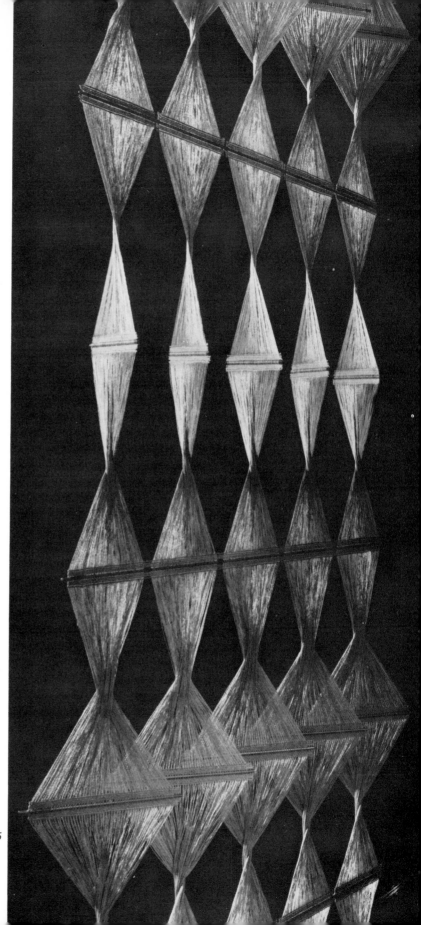

4.5

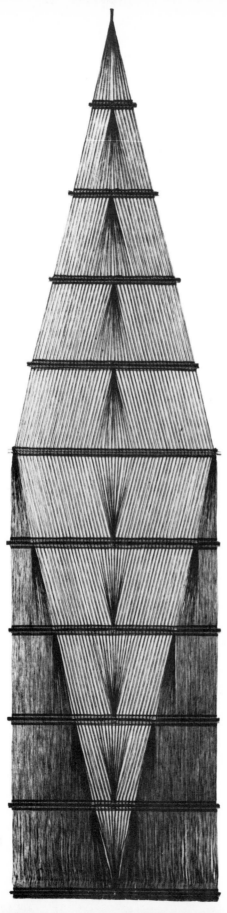

4.6

it may take, the overall tension is always even. Peter Collingwood believes in allowing thread to speak for itself and the latter technique is perfect for highlighting the linear beauty of fine threads ordered with a mathematical logicality.

Other techniques have been and are being explored, but when one thinks of Collingwood's work, the overwhelming picture is of the instantly recognizable, airy, geometric, linear wallhangings, often in whites, naturals and blacks, with the pile and flat rugs coming second and thirdly sprang technique, used in all its variations, from the light and lacy (illustration 4.8) to the close, firm and even, and the three-dimensionally sculptural (illustration 4.10).

Sprang, or Egyptian plaiting, is the name given to a method of twisting together a sheet of vertical threads, held firmly, at top and bottom. Because the threads are held, one row of twisting, at the top, results in a second row being made at the bottom; thus a mirror-repeat effect is achieved, and the work is finished in the middle. There is no weft in this technique.

Peter Collingwood has said, 'I weave because I like weaving. I am happy if others like my weaving sufficiently to buy it, so that I can continue weaving.' This is a typically unpretentious and direct attitude and he has given it a practical basis in developing methods of working which are quick, efficient and flexible, thus keeping the price of work within reasonable limits and therefore within the reach of a greater number of people than can sometimes afford art works. 'Art works' is a term which he would abhor and, in fact, on another occasion he has said, apropos *liking* to weave, 'other motivations, though sounding less selfish, do not apply', and he stoutly denies that he is an 'artist'. If not, then of what does artistry consist? The abstract organization of the textural and graphic elements of the design in any one of his wallhangings can refresh the mind and release the imagination. The simplicity of his verbal statements could mislead as to the complexity, depth and breadth of his intellect.

Peter Collingwood's work is seen at exhibitions worldwide; in 1969, he was also granted an unprecedented accolade in Britain: an exhibition of his work, together with Hans Coper, the ceramist, at the Victoria and Albert Museum, London. British galleries are notoriously slow to recognize media other than that of the painter and sculptor, and this was recognition indeed. In 1974 he was awarded the Order of the British Empire.

He is, perhaps, a bridge between two worlds, that of the artist/craftsman and the museum-researcher. Of these two worlds, he says, 'I know that each can enrich the other, though they often distrust each other and tend to speak different languages.'

He spends the major portion of his daily working time weaving. He does not often have assistants; having perfected fast techniques, with which he is prepared to produce 'limited editions' of his designs, he keeps production within his own hands. Being a solitary, quiet, contemplative, studious man, this method is the obvious one for him.

Peter Collingwood has written three books, all definitive works, which stem from his analytical approach to textile constructions and his wish to share the results of his research with others. *Techniques of Rug Weaving* was published by Faber & Faber in 1967, *The Techniques of Sprang* by the same publishers in 1974. In 1975 he was awarded a Crafts Advisory Committee grant in order to research for a book on tablet (card) weaving.

Finally, Peter Collingwood is a valued influence at textile conferences and seminars worldwide, especially in the United States, but he purposely limits the time and energy he will give to teaching and he is most certainly not a 'committee man'. His absorption with thread, the loom, and the study of and research into textile constructions is the core of what he is about, and he will not allow the continued dialogue to be too often interrupted.

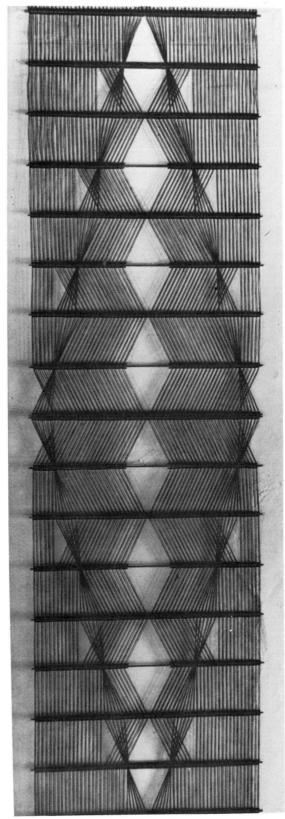

4.6 Macrogauze 35 *(1968), 210cm × 50cm (7ft × 20in); black linen, stainless steel rod*

4.7 Macrogauze 46, *50cm × 160cm (20in × 5ft 5in); black linen, stainless steel rod*

4.7

47

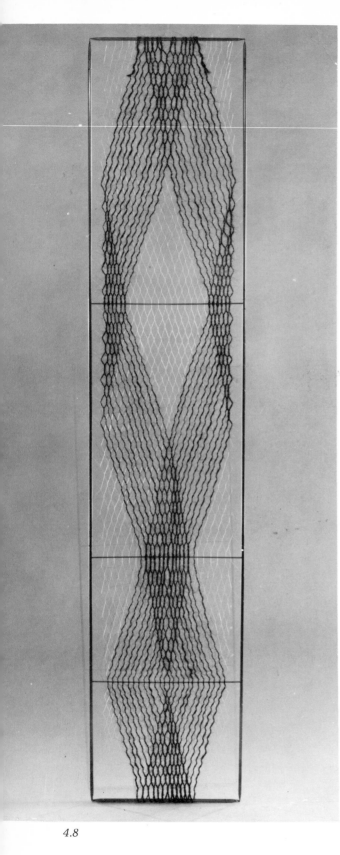

4.8

4.9

1 Prayer in an Eastern Garden *(1973) by Geraldine Brock, 150cm × 165cm (5ft × 5ft 6in); tapestry woven with knotted pile (property of the Department of the Environment)*

2 *Tapestry (1970) by Robert Mabon; linen warp; linen, jute and sisal weft; unglazed stoneware fungoid forms*

3 Bathers *(1976) by Unn Sönju, 180cm × 170cm (6ft × 5ft 8in)*

4 Le Rouge et Le Noir *(1976) by Kathleen Mc-Farlane, 240cm × 366cm (8ft × 12ft); weaving, winding and crochet*

1

2

3

4

5 *One of two tapestries for the Guildhall School of Music, Barbican, London (1977) by Alec Pearson*
240 × 330cm (8ft × 11ft); wool on linen

4.10

4.8 Screen, *195cm × 45cm (6ft 6in × 15in);
horsehair and monofilament nylon, using
sprang technique*

4.9 Macrogauze 86, *84cm × 220cm
(2ft 9in × 7ft 3in)*

4.10 *Detail of Sprang space-hanging,
300cm × 50cm (10ft × 20in); heavy sisal*

49

Bobbie Cox

DARTINGTON, DEVON

Bobbie Cox was born in East Anglia in 1930, but has spent most of her adult life in Devon. From 1945 to 1951 she studied to be an artist and teacher at the Bath Academy of Art, and then embarked upon an art teaching career, combined with her own work, first at Totnes High School, then at the Bath Academy of Art and at Dartington College of Art until 1974. In 1974 she ceased regular teaching to concentrate on weaving, and teaches now only occasionally.

She has always used a variety of media, both flat and three-dimensional, as well as paint. She also holds a great respect for the traditional and primitive craftsman and his handling of materials. Her interest in the use of wool began as long ago as the 1950s, during a visit to Greece where she saw people preparing wool – washing, dyeing and spinning it for weaving. She learned from them and found later that this was a medium which she found both personally satisfying and one which had great potential in the teaching situation. The raw material was available, the equipment simple and the process one which could continue alongside other activities, even the domestic, and therefore could be an unbroken, ongoing experience. Although the weaving and spinning processes are laborious and ones from which modern machines usually relieve us, she finds that she can achieve textures and qualities in handspun wool not obtainable by other methods and which for her make it an expressive material.

In 1973 she travelled extensively in India with her husband, returning there again in 1975 to collect material for an exhibition on the Indian poet, Rabindranath Tagore, which included objects in daily use made by craftsmen in West Bengal. Both these journeys extended her longstanding interest and knowledge of indigenous craftsmen and how they work.

5.1

Her first tapestries were thought of as paintings, the designs evolving through drawings or maquettes and applied to scale to the weaving. She was concerned with the horizontal and vertical structure of weaving and how it could play a part in the design; the tapestries in turn influenced her drawing and painting.

At this point she learned the mechanics of photography, thus making an important extension to her means of recording and methods of designing. One of her sources of inspiration where the camera was particularly useful was in studying the landscape of the quarries of Dartmoor and later the marble quarries of Italy and limestone ones of Provence. In these it was possible to record and compare the natural versus manmade landscapes; strata, rock faces

5.1 *Bobbie Cox*

5.2 *Two views of the artist's studio at Dartington in Devon*

5.2

5.3

5.4

and the effect of light on textured surfaces (illustrations 5.3, 5.6). Her work became more austere with the use of monotone and low relief and more concerned with organic versus manmade shapes. This encouraged her to experiment with different methods of weaving and to explore the different qualities of wool and methods of spinning. For this series mainly natural coloured wools were used. Everyday objects also provided source-material both as starting points and to solve problems, such as the folds in a piece of crumpled paper, a knitted saucepan cleaner, the undoing of a parcel, or fields being ploughed seen from the kitchen window (illustrations 5.5, 5.7, 5.8).

She then became interested in banners, their function and aspect interested her; they could hang free, enrich, give colour and have symbolism, however abstract. She was fascinated by the possibilities of their use in contemporary buildings where their textural weight and warmth and handmade irregularities could make a significant contribution to the world of cement, glass and mechanized units. Her works, for both large buildings and the domestic situation, ceased to be severely rectangular, not so detailed in content but more concerned with proportion, projection and colour, so that the works had various aspects to offer the observer (illustration 5.9). From these banners emerged the present ongoing series called *Coat of Many Colours* (colour plate 8). In these she has departed even further from the rectangle into strips, flaps, folds, turn-backs and spaces.

The construction of these three-dimensional pieces was fully worked out beforehand. The warps were often multi-layered, in order to allow the forms to grow out of the original construction, rather than have parts added on afterwards. A preconception of their behaviour when released from

5.3 Fantiscritti *(1972), 50cm × 50cm (20in × 20in); white wool with pink and ochre wool inset*

5.4 Marble Relief *(1972), 50cm × 50cm (20in × 20in); white and grey natural wools*

5.5 Turned Earth: Dartmoor Winter, Merrivale *(1976), 50cm × 76cm (20in × 30in); natural wools*

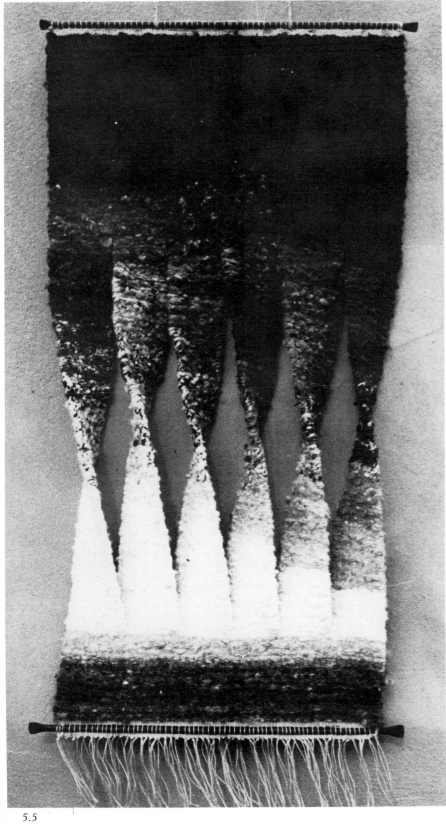

5.5

5.6

5.7

5.8

5.6 Granite Relief: Lee Moor, Dartmoor
*(1975), 84cm × 152cm (35in × 60in);
natural wools handspun and plied*

5.7 Woven Form *(1977), 50cm × 76cm
(20in × 30in); natural wools*

5.8 Turned Earth: Merrivale, Dartmoor
*(1976), 76cm × 147cm (30in × 58in);
natural wools*

5.9 Red Rocket *(1976), 80cm × 240cm
(32in × 8ft); wool*

the tension of the loom was an essential factor in the design process. She found, however, that for details such as surface texture and pattern, allowance for improvisation produced the most satisfactory end results. Working in the medium of weaving, Bobbie Cox admits that she is conscious of a need for restraint in her work – the progress is slower than the flow of ideas, and she is aware of a risk that the end product can become overloaded in content.

She works with wools from local sheep, which is plentiful. Her studio, attached to her home, is equipped with vertical tapestry frames and the floor is heaped with wool, spun, unspun, natural or dyed; she paints with wool.

It is important to her that her work is hung within reach so that people can enjoy the tactile as well as the visual pleasures. For the present *Coat* series her whole method of designing has changed, becoming more constructional, broader in idea, leaving opportunities for 'happenings' to occur in the process of weaving which cannot be preconceived, such as the response of the weaving to its own weight, bulk and the effect of gravity as it grows. She is conscious of the weaving as something that comes to life as it progresses, organic in construction as well as conception. She says

> The end product becomes a dialogue between the idea, the method, the material and the process . . .
> while the design and the practical agitate each other to create forms which stretch my known techniques into the unknown and while the making of each piece is a risky affair, I am excited to continue weaving. I don't see the chronology of my work as being a 'progress', more a progression of thought and exploration, continuous and always unfinished. Weaving is so slow it may take several weeks or months to make each piece and each direction can take years to explore and assess – at the end of which I may return to something left behind as a new starting point.

5.9

Fionna Geddes

EDINBURGH

Fionna Geddes was born in Glasgow in 1949. She began her fine-art training with a foundation year at Newcastle College of Art in 1968 and then studied drawing and painting at Edinburgh College of Art.

It was during this latter period that she began to be interested in the textile medium, finding it both a fascination in itself and also a fluid vehicle by which to express her ideas, which were essentially those of a painter. She gained her Diploma in Art in 1973 and then continued into a postgraduate year at Edinburgh when she worked almost entirely in tactile terms – terms of a highly personal and extremely subtle nature. Coming to textile as she did, untutored in textile technique, she brought to it a fresh and appreciative eye.

6.1

As a result of her post-graduate work she was awarded a travelling scholarship with which she journeyed to Spain and Morocco. Of this journey she says 'It was a sensuous experience both in sight and sound and it reinforced my previous interest in bleached and natural colour and in the "rawness" of materials'. Later she was awarded a Visual Arts 'Awards to Artists' Bursary by the Scottish Arts Council. She now teaches drawing and painting part-time at Edinburgh College of Art, and spends the major portion of her time working from her Edinburgh Studio.

Her works are simple and immensely subtle, generally in whites and naturals. They are statements about the essence of textile in its most fragile, ephemeral and delicate manifestations. They are precious fragments, and have all the reference and depth of pieces of historic textile. They do not dominate the observer but quietly draw one into a close and intimate observation.

They are structures of 'mixed media' in the widest sense. She uses earth, plaster, cane, wood, bamboo, Japanese paper, fibres, already-knitted and woven fabrics and simple techniques like lashing, plain weaving, binding and wrapping, all welded together with adhesives, resin bonding and paint.

She is very much concerned with the natural state of materials, and wishes to create a tension between the materials and the process, which she sees as both sensual and intellectual. Her work explores, for example, the horizontal and vertical rhythms of bamboo and twine, which are often used as weft with a cotton warp.

6.1 *Fionna Geddes*

6.2 Yggdrasil *(1975), 165cm × 116cm (5ft 6in × 3ft 10in); white lace, plaster, earth, acrylic resin and oil paint. Yggdrasil has three interpretations: the Scandinavian world-tree (the ash-tree which supports the universe), the theme of rebirth, and the theme of the reunion of opposites*

6.3 *Detail of* Section 3

6.4 Section 3 *(1977), 200cm × 96cm (6ft 8in × 3ft 2in); woven cotton warp; weft of Japanese paper, straw, acrylic resin, balsa wood, jute, wool and linen*

56

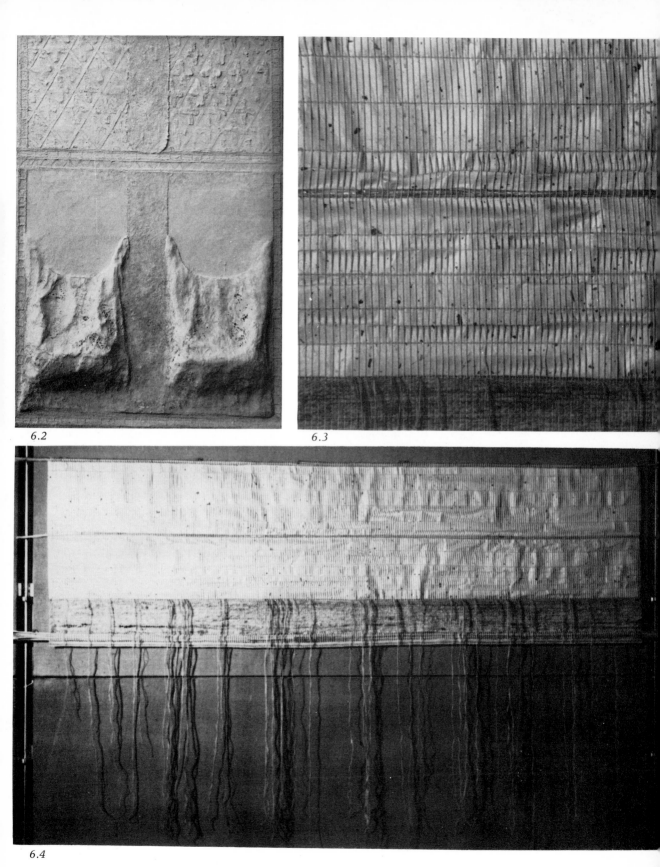

6.2

6.3

6.4

6.5

She begins by confining them within a geometric form – the square flat plane – then gradually allows the concealed energy inherent within them to break free and revert to its natural state. The square grid with which the piece starts is covered and uncovered, then fragmented and destroyed.

One of her methods is to paint in oils onto a cotton duck canvas, using a base coat of saturated primary colour straight from the tube, with over-layers of light grey. The primary colours are sensed through the grey, and often an edge of base colour is left at the bottom of the canvas to give a literal clue as to the development of the process, and the flatness of the original plane. Vertical warps suspended in front of the structure complete the 'optical weave' effect created by texturing and furrowing the painted surface.

She combines the processes of painting and weaving with other techniques, such as photography, etching and lithography. Her work is non-representational and non-illusionist, and she relates the conception of the piece very much to the gallery space and environment which it will eventually occupy.

Ken Dingwall wrote at the time of her 'New Work 1977' exhibition in Edinburgh: 'The growth of Geddes's work has been marked by the development of the tactile sense always present in her painting, toward an extremely sensitive response to a wide range of natural materials, earth, straw, bamboo and flax.'

Her interest in the textural sensations of paint and collage have led to a greater awareness of the physical properties of materials, to a sense of wanting to be held by these properties and by the simple processes needed to put them together. Weaving, knotting and binding are universal functional acts she touches on. The simple limits of the grid of weaving have provided a framework to improvise against. The act of making is important to her, the manual act stimulating the emotional or intellectual attitudes in the work.

Her work is included in important International Tapestry Shows but she still thinks of herself as a painter. Explorations into other areas are seen by her as situations which will expand her sensibilities in paint handling and language. These explorations are intended to remove any dependency on figuration; rather than imitate, she wishes to organize matter to create its own energy.

6.5 Section 2 (1977), 200cm × 7cm (6ft 8in × 3in); woven cotton warp; weft of Japanese paper, straw, acrylic resin, jute and balsa wood

6.6 Intersection 2 (1977), 30cm × 30cm (12in × 12in); straw, sisal, plaster, earth, acrylic resin, sawdust; one of a series of 16 panels

6.7 Intersection (1977), 120cm × 114cm (4ft × 3ft 9in); straw, sisal, plaster, earth, acrylic resin, sawdust

6.8 Growth (1975), 120cm × 120cm (4ft × 4ft); knitted wool and acrylic, plaster, acrylic resin and oil paint (property of the Scottish Arts Council)

6.6

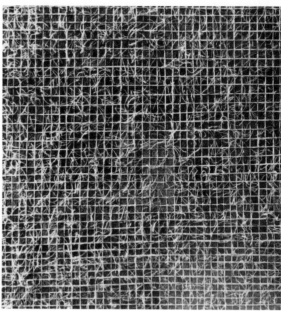

6.7

6.8

Myriam Gilby

ESSEX

Myriam Gilby was born in Yercand, South India, in 1929. From 1947 to 1959 she attended the Regent Street Polytechnic, London, where her concerns were mainly drawing and sculpture. She then undertook an Art Teachers Diploma at Goldsmith's College of Art, London. She entered the teaching profession, first teaching art and craft at Whitecroft County Secondary School at Bolton in Lancashire, where she remained for five years, and from 1957 to the present day as Head of the Art and Design Department at Lucton County Girls' School in Essex. She now also teaches adults and works in her own studio at Buckhurst Hill.

From her sculptural training she developed also a concern with painting, mainly in oils. She has always been preoccupied with water, the movement of the sea, the strata of rocks, and landscape. In 1966, as a result of casting around for another medium, one which would combine some of the qualities of painting and sculpture, i.e. three-dimensionality and colour, she began to attend Ruth Hurle's weaving classes at the Stanhope Institute, London. From then on her medium has become more and more totally textile. In the following years much of her textile contact was to come through the London Weavers Guild and it was an Association of Guilds Exhibition which was the catalyst for one of her largest pieces of work, *Seadrift* (illustration 7.5).

Her concern is always with life and movement, particularly of the sea. Her works have great flowing vitality and three-dimensionality. They are shaped and pierced, they twist, curve and fold. Ground weaves are generally simple tapestry with a wool weft, but additionally such techniques are used as will best give life and form to the work, twining, binding, finger weaving, soumak, bound warps and wefts, looping and tufting, knotting, netting,

7.1

crochet, knitting, embroidery, areas of double cloth and the addition of extra warp ends. Many of the techniques are the result of study in the ethnological museums. Lately a completely three-dimensional method has been developed based on a netting structure.

Materials used, in either fibre or yarn form and, as often as not dyed by herself, are wool, horsehair, mohair, camel-hair, sisal, jute, hemp, ropes, string, packing twine and agricultural binder-twine. Many of her materials come from the stationer, the ships-chandler or the nurseryman; she also incorporates materials like rags and metal waste.

7.1 *Myriam Gilby in her studio*

7.2 Strata 1 *(1976), 210cm × 140cm (7ft × 4ft 6in); tapestry techniques with bound wefts, soumak embroidery (collection of Mrs Dennyer, Essex)*

7.3 Winter Sea *(1975), 165cm × 120cm (5ft 6in × 4ft); tapestry base with layered warp (collection of Dr and Mrs Harrison, Glasgow)*

7.4 Red Composition *(1970), 240cm × 180cm (5ft × 6ft); hanging warps in horsehair and sisal with wool ball shapes*

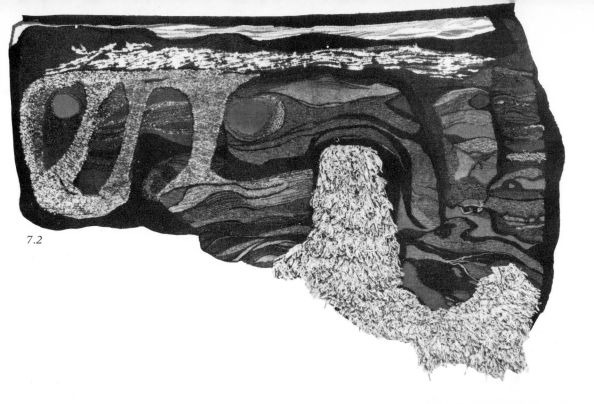

7.2

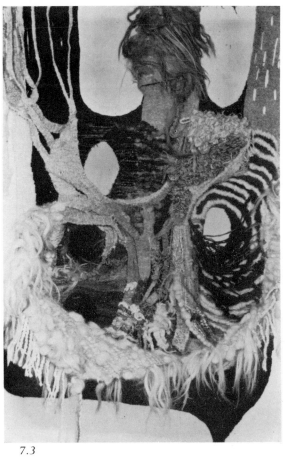

7.3

7.4

7.5

7.6

7.7

7.5 Seadrift *(1972), 240cm × 360cm (8ft × 12ft); tapestry base using a variety of looped techniques; some natural dyes*

7.6 *Detail of* Seadrift

7.7 Textile Sculpture *(1977), 180cm × 140cm × 91cm (6ft × 4ft 6in × 3ft); the structure is based on a net; wool over a sisal net*

63

The pieces of work are rich in texture and lustre. Light affects each material in a different way, sometimes bouncing off the surface, at other times being absorbed. Matt surfaces are contrasted with glossy or harsh areas. The way light penetrates fibres is used to advantage: wool, massed in a heavily textured area, forms rich shadows, while the same technique, using a man-made or vegetable fibre, has the opposite effect – that of successive layers of reflected light.

As with most weavers, Myriam Gilby finds there is always the problem of not enough studio space – and as a result large pieces of work have to be woven in sections. It is not possible to use a conventional tapestry loom as it is difficult to wind heavily-textured areas around the cloth bar. So, again, using ideas from the ethnological museums, a loom was designed and built by Myriam Gilby herself for the specific problems involved. Later this wooden loom was replaced by one made from builder's scaffolding. Some pieces are constructed on a warp-weighted loom; the opportunities for surface movement within the construction are consequently greatly enhanced.

In order to ensure that the design fits together when the separate sections of weaving are assembled the loom is marked off at 30cm (12in) intervals along the cloth bar and uprights. The designs always conform to these measurements, no matter how apparently free the weaving might appear to be. Thought has to be given to creating design features which distract the eye away from the joins in the work rendering them unobtrusive.

She has become known for her weaving since about 1970 when she first began to exhibit. Most of her works are quite large and she visualizes them as hung in public buildings. Certainly their strong characteristics and the vibrancy and movement within them demand adequate breathing-space. She says of her weaving, 'I prefer to carry out a hanging with the minimum of pre-planning. I like to evolve my ideas as the work progresses thereby sustaining a high degree of mental tension. Weaving techniques pose their own problems and dictate solutions which, in turn, affect the design'. Of her mental processes, 'Ideas can remain dormant for several years before the right circumstances occur to use them. As a student on holiday in Cornwall, I made water-colour studies of the surging and foaming of the sea against rocks; the water-colours went in the waste-bin – the qualities which gripped my imagination at the time were not ones I could use in paint'.

She now uses a camera as freely and as often as she does a sketch-book, also photographs, magazine-cuttings and found objects.

She spins many of her own yarns, not on a wheel nor a drop-spindle, but on a spool winder which works on the same principle as the 'great wheel' or 'walking wheel', allowing the production of heavy, chunky, slubby yarns. She blends dyed fibres together in the carding and spinning, throws yarns of many sorts into the same dye-bath to achieve varied results, tie-dyes yarns, and generally adopts an attitude in which the concept is the centre of concern, the methods of achieving it follow.

In 1976 she wrote *Free Weaving* (Pitman) which encapsulates her idea and methods of working.

7.8 Textile Sculpture *(1977), 180cm × 140cm × 91cm (6ft × 4ft 6in × 3ft); wool over a sisal net*

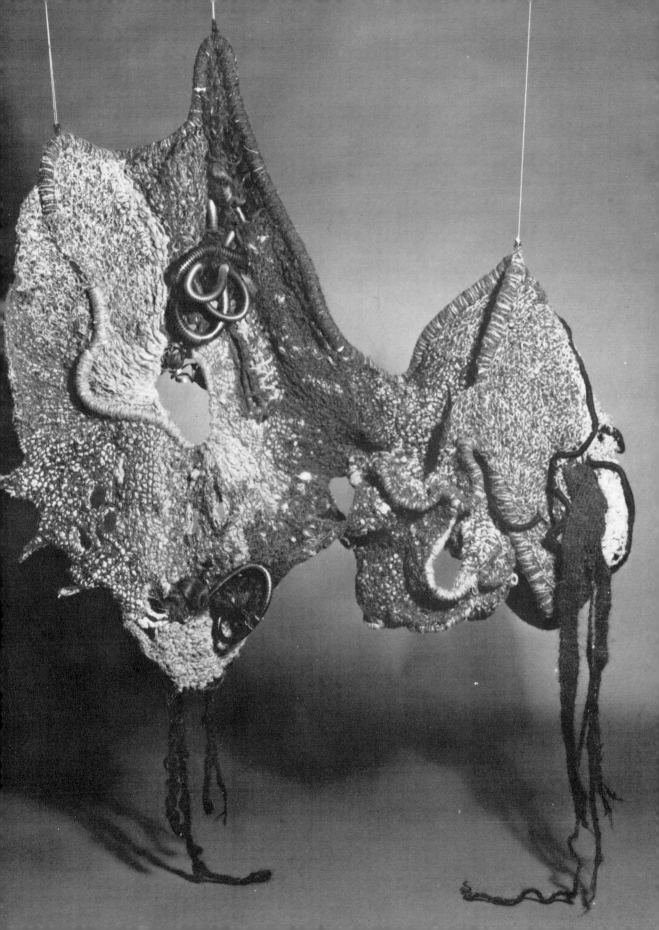

Maureen Hodge

EDINBURGH

Maureen Hodge was born at Perth, on the River Tay in eastern Scotland, in 1941. She entered Edinburgh College of Art in 1959 and studied for her diploma in stained glass under Sax Shaw, following Archie Brennan by two years.

Upon qualifying in 1962 Archie Brennan had been offered a contract to teach in the College and that session the tapestry section began in a very unofficial way with one student – Maureen Hodge; and so the evolution of a series of remarkable tapestry artists had started. She was awarded an Andrew Grant post-graduate scholarship and abandoned stained glass completely to concentrate on tapestry. Shortly after leaving the College she produced *Winterwood IV* (illustration 8.3), a superb and complete textile statement.

For the following nine years she worked with Archie Brennan at the Edinburgh Tapestry Co. She continued to design and weave her own work, and during the last three years of the period she also assisted Archie Brennan in his teaching in the College Tapestry Department as the numbers of students increased.

Her first tapestries had been flat and traditional but from her post-graduate year this developed into textural hangings, many based on landscape or trees and forests (*Winterwood*, illustration 8.3). From there she moved into a series of three-dimensional 'tents'. This series epitomizes the theme that underlies much of her work, which is the idea of a 'secret', something hinted at but not revealed. *From her tower . . .* (illustration 8.2) is the first of the tents and is both a mysterious and an ambiguous three-dimensional hanging structure. She was very influenced by the Middle Ages and lettering plays an important part in the whole, both in the import of the words and their graphic significance. She finds words fascinating: 'Even a single word can have an immense emotive capa-

8.1

city and the possibilities between the apparent and the hidden meaning can have so many stimulating implications.' Many of the early tents were muted and sombre but opened up to reveal bright jewel-like interiors usually containing lettering. One was lined with soft white fleece and had a poem on the outside of the door flap. The last tent, produced in 1974, was the most austere and the least self-indulgent (illustration 8.4). It could not be entered, revealing when opened only sheet aluminium in which the onlooker was distorted reflected. She says, 'This was the ultimate and really secret and closed tent – or a completely empty one – a void.'

8.1 *Maureen Hodge in her studio, 1977*

8.2 From her tower whilst half awake he answers *(1970), 300cm × 70cm diameter (10ft × 28in diameter); wool tapestry weave with tassels, chaining, plaiting knotting and bells; greys and blacks*

8.2

8.3

In 1973 it was decided to appoint a full-time head of the Tapestry Department at Edinburgh College of Art and as Archie Brennan did not wish to give up his work at the Edinburgh Tapestry Co., Maureen Hodge left her work there and took up the post at the College.

More or less coinciding with her move into full-time lecturing, the tents series came to an end, and the 'Hill' series started, and with them a change in emphasis in technique. She now became engrossed with the relationship between an object and its setting and this became crystallized on the hill/sky idea. *Haystack Hill* (illustration 8.5) was produced in 1975, a totally textural, visual and tactile experience. She then moved on, becoming less interested in deep texture and more concerned with marks and graphic images, as in *A Hill for my Friend* made in 1976 (illustration 8.6). She says,

> I really weave just for myself (and perhaps one other person). If people like what I do that's fine, if they don't – they may be right but it doesn't really matter to me. I am trying to resolve something for myself, a balance, a tension, an idea. Sometimes I may succeed, other times one must try again. There is some technical struggle but this is very insignificant compared to the mental battle to achieve one small step towards greater self-knowledge and through that greater understanding of one's place in

the 'scheme of things' and from this some concrete expression in aesthetic terms. At the back of it all is the riddle which has no answer. One can feel that one is paring away the layers, but the kernel is never revealed.

Maureen Hodge is master of whatever idea and techniques she is using at the moment. All problems are resolved before and at the moment of weaving, leaving nothing unsatisfactory or unfinished, and presenting the viewer in every case with an object for constant contemplation.

She does not like working to commission. She feels that working for another person, or place, introduces factors which for her muddy the issues with which she is grappling. She is therefore content to be involved in education as it removes any need for her to sell her tapestries. She is a dedicated teacher and demands unremitting hard work from her students. The work coming from the school is a constant affirmation of the skill of herself and the staff.

Finally, she writes of tapestry in general, 'The end result should be something peculiar to tapestry and impossible in any other medium' and, of her own work, 'The meanings in my pieces of work are contained more in the mood created than in specific incident. I weave to produce the expression of a thought, a memory or an emotion. If I could do this solely in words, or any other way, I would not weave.'

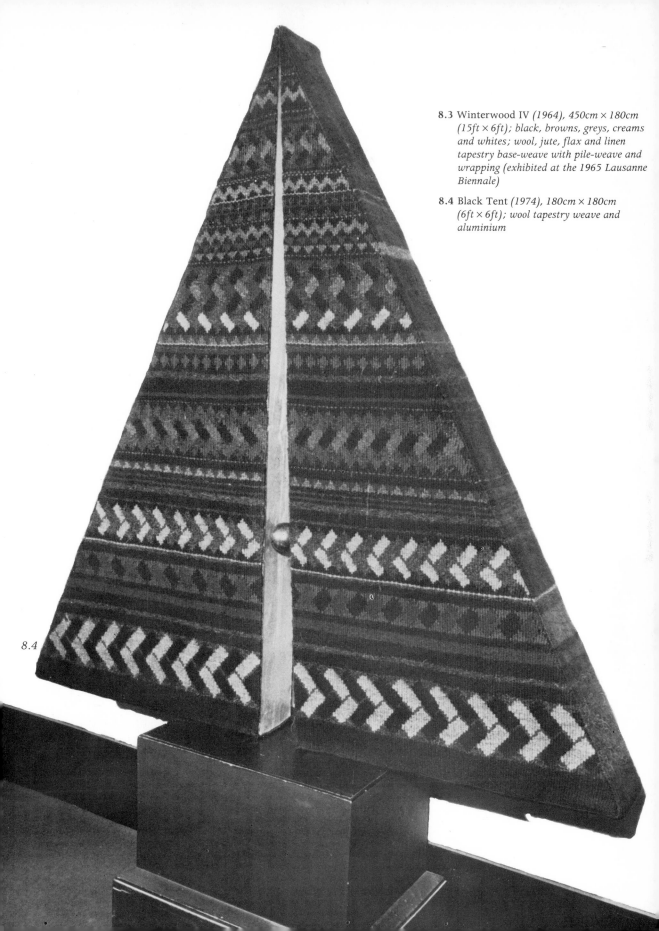

8.3 Winterwood IV *(1964), 450cm × 180cm
(15ft × 6ft); black, browns, greys, creams
and whites; wool, jute, flax and linen
tapestry base-weave with pile-weave and
wrapping (exhibited at the 1965 Lausanne
Biennale)*

8.4 Black Tent *(1974), 180cm × 180cm
(6ft × 6ft); wool tapestry weave and
aluminium*

8.4

8.5 Haystack Hill *(1975), 195cm × 195cm (6ft 6in × 6ft 6in); Turkish and Persian knot, cut and uncut in flax, jute, sisal and gold thread; tapestry and knotting*

8.6 A Hill for my Friend *(1976), 200cm ×*
175cm (6ft 8in × 5ft 10in); wool, mohair,
cotton and linen tapestry

Robert Mabon

BUCKINGHAMSHIRE

Robert Mabon was born in 1929 in County Durham. He was encouraged to take an interest in craft work of various kinds when he was quite young. At school his ambitions were directed towards architecture and stage design, and both of these have remained of great interest to him, although, during the crucial examination years, mathematics became his prime subject. A preliminary year at Camberwell School of Art introduced him to the 'delights and frustrations of potting' which has remained a strong passion and intermittent activity. This was followed by an interior design course at the Central School of Art, London.

He spent the first ten years of his professional life designing shops, interiors and furniture, firstly in the contracts department of a retail furnisher, then in an architectural practice and, finally, with an exhibition designer. He then moved into the teaching sphere, lecturing in interior and furniture design at High Wycombe College.

During most of this early period much time and energy had been expended on 'building a house, planting a garden, designing and producing plays, building sets, making costumes, designing carpets for industry, making pots, going to the opera, singing madrigals and visiting Greek monasteries'. He finally came to regard his life-style as a dissipation of his energies and, in 1965, decided to give up both teaching and work at the drawing-board in order to try to weld his work and his general interests into a homogeneous whole. He began to concentrate on work of a personal and direct nature which would include the making as well as the designing process, without necessarily being confined to one medium. In essence this was a move away from general concern with the complete interior to a more detailed consideration of the interior's individual

9.1

elements – elements needing direct practical involvement, and not necessarily confining him to one medium.

Textile techniques had long been of great interest to him but he had never attempted them seriously. Now, he built a simple upright two-shaft loom and some frames and started to weave. He is largely self-taught as a weaver, obtaining some help from books, but mostly through 'trial and error', discovering problems, possibilities and solutions himself and developing his own philosophy through working in the textile medium.

He started making rugs and wallhangings in tapestry weave in simple stripes and geometric designs. Then, to achieve a greater range of texture, he began combining tapestry with knotted pile and soumak (in which the weft yarn is carried *around* each warp end). The desire to weave rugs and then tapestries and wallhangings of a more distinctive and complex character, non-geometric and non-repetitive, led to

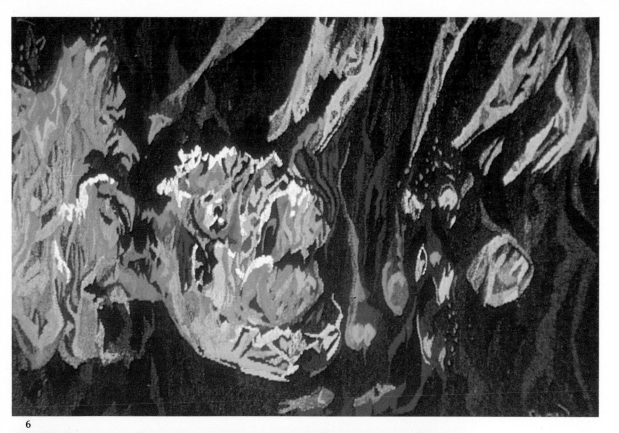

6

7

6 Earth *(1968) by Sax Shaw, 165cm × 120cm (5ft 6in × 4ft), (Leo Rothschild Collection)*

7 *Detail of* **Boudoir Bat** *(1974) by Maggie Riegler, 225cm × 105cm (7ft 6in × 3ft 6in); tapestry knotting, tasselling, wrapping (collection of the Scottish Arts Council)*

8 Coat of Many Colours 7 *(1977) by Bobbie Cox, 165cm × 210cm (5ft. 6in × 7ft); dyed wools*

9 Transition Spectrum Permutation *(1976) by Ann Sutton, 244cm × 244cm (8ft × 8ft); wool and nylon monofilament (collection of City of Leeds Museum, Lotherton Hall)*

8

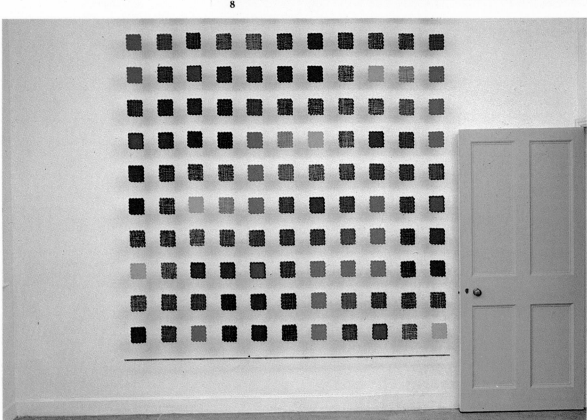

9

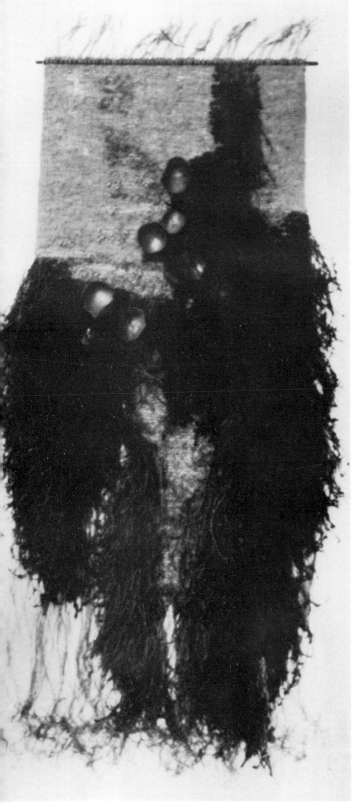

9.3

9.1 *Robert Mabon at the loom*

9.2 Black and Orange Landscape *(1972),
142cm × 76cm (4ft 8in × 2ft 6in); sisal
warp; sisal and unspun jute weft; sisal
pile; glazed stoneware fungoid forms*

9.3 Rug *(1968), 168cm × 107cm (5ft 6in ×
3ft 6in); linen warp; wool weft; double
weave (collection of W G Whear)*

9.2

9.4

9.5

the use of a double-weave technique on the double-shed principle. In this, every third warp end is not entered through a heddle; it therefore divides the shed into two when the shafts are moved. The pattern is achieved by weaving with a contrasting weft in each shed; changeover of weft and colour between the two sheds can be made at any point (illustration 9.3). The technique is slow but extremely flexible in design, and such, in fact, were its almost limitless possibilities that he felt it necessary to beware of producing effects which, though technically fascinating, may not work well as pattern on the floor.

In 1966 he was much stimulated by the exhibition of Polish tapestries at the Grabowski Gallery, London, and acknowledges a debt to the work of Abakanowicz, Sadley, Buic, Beutlich and Di Mare in giving dramatic indication of the possibilities of weaving as a truly expressive medium. He is also conscious of the influence of the painters De Stael, Zack, Tapies and Hoyland, and the sculptor Bertoia. The first rugs and tapestries had been woven in wool on cotton warps using a combination of plain tapestry weave and knotted pile, but now he began to experiment with the use of different wefts (wool, cotton, sisal, horsehair, unspun jute, etc.) on cotton, linen, sisal or camel hair warps using different techniques – tapestry, plain weave, pile, gauze (in which warp ends are made to cross over each other), weft floats, distorted weft, etc. – to achieve richness and range of texture within one piece (illustration 9.4). Another technique developed at this period was an extremely open plain weave with linen, sisal and unspun jute weft wandering across a fine linen warp, with denser areas of close weaving and sisal pile such as seen in *Winged Form* (illustration 9.7). These were woven on frames, thus making the whole capable of visual appraisal during weaving,

9.6   9.7

and the open weaving was fixed with PVA medium before removal. Concurrently, some three-dimensional pieces were produced, either by manipulating, sewing and stiffening woven sections after removal from the loom and with macramé additions, or wholly in macramé knotting. The use of armatures was, whenever possible, avoided, an attempt being made to use gravity and suspension as factors in achieving form.

His parallel interest in potting led to some very interesting and beautiful wall-hangings, three-dimensional hangings and standing forms, combining the two media in different ways, but always the two seeming indissoluble. Pinched stoneware fungoid shapes were incorporated in the weaving as an integral part of the design (illustration 9.5). Other pieces were predominantly ceramic with outcrops of sisal (illustration 9.6). Although the materials and techniques in weaving and potting are

utterly different, Robert Mabon finds areas of common ground between the two, both in his attitude to the use of the material and in the imagery which has evolved. Much cross-fertilization has taken place and, at times, it has been possible to see an unbroken progression from an all-textile piece to an all-ceramic one. Working in

9.4 Pink Rockface *(1968), 76cm × 53cm (2ft 6in × 1ft 9in); linen warp; wool, sisal and unspun jute weft; sisal pile*

9.5 Yellow Fissure *(1969), 117cm × 61cm (3ft 10in × 1 ft); linen warp; linen, unspun jute and sisal weft; sisal pile; glazed stoneware fungoid forms*

9.6 *Untitled relief (1972); handbuilt stoneware with dry ash glaze; knotted sisal*

9.7 Winged Form *(1969), 99cm × 56cm (3ft 3in × 1ft 10in); linen warp; linen, sisal and unspun jute weft; sisal pile*

75

9.8

demands. By 1972 textures had become extremely shaggy and outlines irregular, and gradually he became aware of a need for a more disciplined approach. The pinched fungoid and textile technique was becoming a mere formula and he did not wish to go on repeating it. He felt that too much reliance on the superficially decorative qualities of the medium and on seductive textures and 'happy accidents' could become a means of disguising undisciplined thinking, weak form and lack of commitment. He entered into a long period of reassessment and experiment during which, trapped in a labyrinth of doubt and self-criticism, he allowed very little work to survive.

For him the medium of weaving has particular features which make it both stimulating and frustrating. The woven structure and the textures which can be achieved give great richness and provide an expressive medium with unique qualities, but most techniques are very slow and one must start at one end, completing each section as the work evolves, with no possibility of making corrections. Adherence to a painted cartoon is not the right approach for him as it seems to be using tapestry merely as a means of reproducing a design conceived in another medium, 'a kind of laborious second-hand spontaneity', and yet he feels the need for some preliminary design, however slight, to provide a visual structure on which to build the final design as it evolves on the loom. He is equally aware that too much reliance on spontaneity on the loom can easily lead to a lack of cohesion and commitment, 'an obsession with detail and flabbiness of form'. For him, ideally, the making and designing processes should be simultaneous and completely interdependent, his aim being a total synthesis of image, material and technique, the approach being, in a sense, like that of a painter; the woven structure and the craftsmanship involved in producing it are vital as means to achieving the total entity that he desires, not as ends in themselves.

More recent work shows the same concern with contrasts of texture as formerly, but more restrained (illustration 9.10). Areas of tapestry in sisal or wool are contrasted with areas of twill or satin weave, weaves which give heightened

two quite different media obviously has its difficulties and problems but he has always disliked the idea of crafts being forced into rigidly separate categories and considers almost any mixture of media to be potentially fruitful.

In 1971 a large tapestry was commissioned by Trust Houses Forte Ltd – it was an irregularly shaped piece in seven overlapping sections (detail in illustration 9.9), the lower parts in sisal pile, the upper in unspun jute and wool. This was followed in 1972 by another large piece for the same clients, this time a semi-open screen in sisal and jute with areas of plain weaving, gauze weaving and double-sided pile. Apart from these pieces, however, most of his work has been on a fairly domestic-size scale due to the problems of making large pieces speculatively, of working in a very small studio, and of maintaining the vision, impetus and cohesion that a large piece

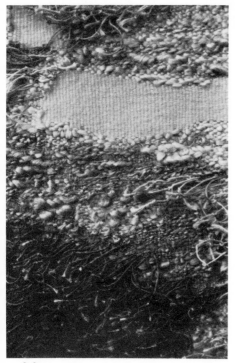

9.9

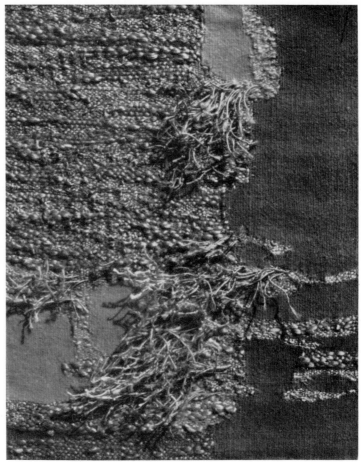

9.10

surface-lustre, in unspun jute or sisal, on warps of linen or sisal. Texture is also achieved by over-twisting yarn or fibre so tightly that it twists and kinks and forms knobs. Colour ranges are more narrow, the greater the contrast of texture the more monochromatic. Yarns are dyed with Procion. Some recent pieces have been in two or more separate panels, the forms continuous but the background colours changing from one panel to the next. Designs often give the illusion of extending beyond the edges of the piece as though a detail of something bigger. Imagery usually suggests a somewhat remote concern with landscape, natural forms and processes of erosion or decay, though always expressed in terms of the medium.

For Robert Mabon the struggle to evolve a method of working which is both a valid vehicle for his imagery and economically feasible goes on. He is an artist plagued with almost paralysing bouts of self-criticism and thus output of work is intermittent, but when he allows them to survive, his works flow and vibrate with his personal and individual translation of the natural world around him.

9.8 *Untitled (1969), 122cm × 76cm (4ft × 2ft 6in); linen warp; linen, sisal and unspun jute weft; sisal pile; glazed stoneware fungoid forms*

9.9 *Detail of a tapestry for Trust Houses Forte (1971), 215cm × 264cm (7ft × 8ft 8in); camel-hair warp; tapestry weave in wool, plain weave in unspun jute and sisal; pile in sisal*

9.10 *Untitled (1971), 69cm × 51cm (2ft 3in × 1ft 8in); camel-hair warp; wool, sisal and unspun jute weft; sisal pile*

Fiona Mathison

EDINBURGH

Fiona Mathison was born in Newcastle, the industrial north-east of England, in 1947, though she has lived most of her life in the borders of Scotland. She studied for her graduate and post-graduate diplomas in the Tapestry Department of the Edinburgh College of Art with Archie Brennan from 1966 to 1971. There she was to find herself much in tune with his philosophy, which was one of utter and total commitment to the medium of tapestry to the point of working day and night – yet detached and wry about its total domination. This attitude often results in work of a satirical nature and in an artist making visual jokes about his or her very slavery to his medium, and it was to prove so with her. However, it was during her student period at Edinburgh at the height of her skills, as they developed, that *Camel* was produced (illustration 10.2) and in this piece of work there was clearly to be seen her present skill and future potential.

To Fiona Mathison, the idea of producing a woven image (the camel bag) of a woven textile object was an amusing one. Presenting it as part of a two-dimensional cut out shape (the camel) extended the joke further. The camel and the bag had to have very different characters, so they were woven on different warps, the camel on grey hair and the bag on cotton, and on different counts of warp threads, 4 to 2·5cm (1in) and 6 to 2·5cm (1in). The whole tapestry was woven all at once, with the rein woven right across the image. The weaving began from the top, upside down, so that the legs could be shaped by pulling in and pushing out the warp threads. The body was shaped by cutting the warps and weaving them as weft, giving a smooth line and a strong edge. The rings from which the camel hangs were worked out at the design stage, since the hanging of the tapestry was an essential part of its textile quality.

From Edinburgh she was accepted at the

10.1

Royal College of Art, London, where she spent a further two years working in tapestry. Here the work became even more 'tongue in cheek'. She deliberately cast away the facile ease of continuing to work with the unquestioning enjoyment in textile seen in *Camel*, and began to produce the ordinary paraphernalia of domestic life in textile terms: three-dimensional objects reproduced in all their detail – unmade beds, sinks, hot-water bottles, but still stemming from her observation of subtle texture contrasts such as a terry towel hung beside a glass-cloth or a rubber hot-water bottle lying on a cotton sheet. It can be assumed that her social comment com-

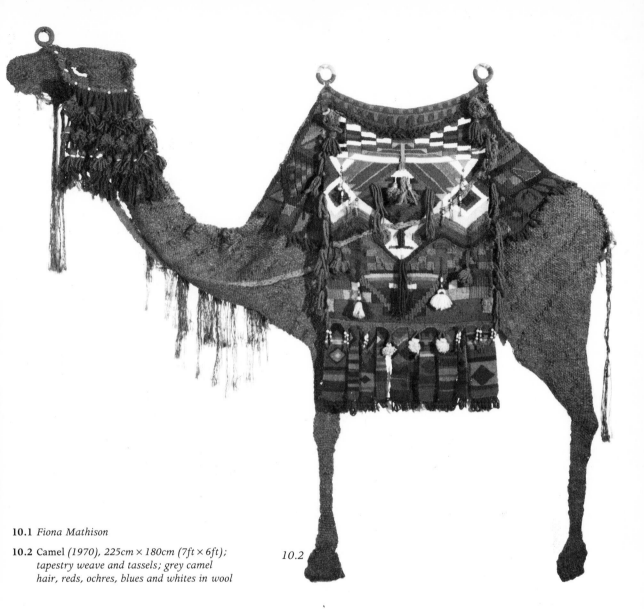

10.1 *Fiona Mathison*

10.2 Camel *(1970), 225cm × 180cm (7ft × 6ft);*
tapestry weave and tassels; grey camel
hair, reds, ochres, blues and whites in wool

10.2

municated itself to others with some force,
as *Who's Been Sleeping in My Bed?*
(illustration 10.3) was exhibited at the 1973
Tapestry Biennale at Lausanne. In this
piece of work she was weaving fabric and
then folding and draping it so that it was
both itself *and* representational.

In order to suggest the different qualities
of the materials – the rigidity of a mattress,
the crispness of a cotton sheet, the softness
of a woollen blanket, the lightness of a
cotton bedspread – each fabric had to be
constructed in a different way to ensure
that they draped differently. This was done
by giving each its own warp and weft
balance, beating down the weft in some

and weaving more loosely in others.
Though the balance of weft to warp varied,
the warp itself was always the same thin
cotton, but varied in warp count and in the
number of ply woven together as one
warp. The technical design was completely worked out beforehand; the stripes
on both the bedcover and the mattress
were arranged to give the impression of
foreshortening. The basic shape was made
of metal strips, joined by bolts, so that it
could collapse and be rolled up, but the
metal was sewn to the underside of the
tapestry so that it was not visible – the bed
'was just there'.

Fiona Mathison is a representational

10.3

artist, even though the objects of her attention, her attitude towards them and her handling of them change along with her intellectual progress. Of her work at this period she said: 'I am as much, if not more, concerned with the accurate representation of the texture of an object, as with its shape, pattern, colour and volume.' She also obviously recognized the accurate representation of everyday objects as a method of taking the rise out of a discipline which she feels is sometimes in danger of taking itself too seriously. This extended into whimsical, cartoon-like tapestries where an inanimate object was given animate characteristics (*H.W. Bottle Esq*).

For four years during her post-graduate studies at Edinburgh and at the Royal College of Art, she worked part-time in the Edinburgh Tapestry Company's studios as a weaver, where Archie Brennan was director and where many students from the college gain invaluable practical experience. Here she underwent the discipline of translating the works of others as well as continuing to work on her own ideas. The Company is unique in its approach to the active and lively part the weaver at the loom has to play in the practical realization of another's concept.

In 1974 she returned to Edinburgh to become a lecturer in tapestry in the department where she had herself trained. She notes this year as a time of reassessment. She began to seek greater flexibility of decision-making during the execution of a piece of work, with less already decided by means of drawings and more happening spontaneously during weaving (something she had hitherto distrusted). In 1975, *Picnic* (illustration 10.4) was the first tapestry for a long time where detail was decided upon during weaving and where she allowed herself, to a certain extent, to rely upon intuition.

The manmade images in the tapestry were carefully worked out beforehand, but she found it impossible to weave the natural landscape in a flat pictorial way since the number of warps needed to achieve such an image would automatically make the subject lose vitality. Thus the materials, raffia, flax and sisal, dyed and natural, had to carry the image. She also found that making the image work as a whole caused certain problems, as the tapestry became

10.3 Who's Been Sleeping in My Bed? *(1973), 315cm × 150cm × 30cm (10ft 6in × 5ft × 1ft); tapestry weave and plain weave, three-dimensional*

10.4 Picnic *(1975), 100cm × 165cm (3ft × 5ft 6in); flat tapestry and pile*

80

10.4

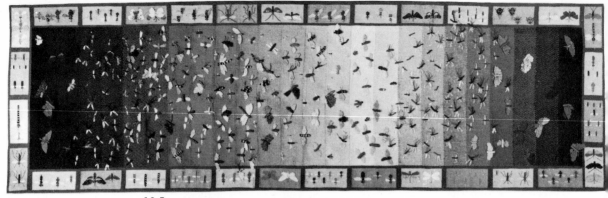

10.5

two separate parts – the strong relief of the landscape and the flat mechanical area of the manmade fabric. Her solution was to introduce a flatter pictorial area at the top of the tapestry and bring in an element of the natural landscape at the bottom.

Also in *Picnic* came the first use (beautifully observed and accurately executed) of insects as part of her vocabulary; these she sees as a delineation of ourselves and our 'civilization'. Since this piece of work, the actual textile fabric she has produced is the fabric of the piece of work itself and not a faithful representation of another fabric or material. It could be said that she has now entered a unified phase of her work; she is less inclined to stand back and joke, and is more content to allow herself to enter into the medium itself; she leaves her social comment to the imagery, and does not work it out with the materials. Her work has become less three-dimensional, more flat and graphic. One has to be alert to appreciate her meanings but, unlike some artists, her titles help and are necessary. *Flies and Half-Truths*, two heads from which are issuing insects, was produced in 1976, and *Patterns of Life and Death*, a technically skilful piece of work, in 1977 (illustrations 10.6, 10.5).

In *Flies and Half-Truths* came the introduction of the human figure. These were not intended to be woven drawings, but a tapestry image, describing only the essential elements of a profile. In the figures, only one material was used, in two thicknesses, and the features were suggested by using cut back lines (ie weaving separate shapes in the same material, so that only the junction of the shapes can be seen). The insects were originally intended to form a tufted carpet, but after weaving several samples it was plain that the image became lost. The final solution was to make the insects issuing from the mouths of the figures in strong relief and for them to recede as they formed the pattern of the rug. This was achieved by whipping over extra floating wefts and adding extra warps for the wings. The background to the figures was critical. It had to move from a glowing red to a grey/black. This was done in a series of arcs woven in varying mixtures of red and grey wool plied together.

Fiona Mathison says, 'For me there is greater flexibility through the medium of weaving than through any other. In what other medium can one create surface and build onto it and give colour, texture and shape all at the same time?' She means what she says, but she is a highly intellectual artist who probably could have been equally articulate in words as in visuals. Having discovered the delights of the textile medium, she was unwilling to drown in its pleasures in case her mind never surfaced again, and has spent a good part of her formative years doing battle. The contentions over which the battle has been fought are now being resolved, but struggle always will continue to be part of her questioning attitudes.

10.5 Patterns of Life and Death *(1977), 256cm × 75cm (8ft 6in × 2ft 6in); flat tapestry*

10.6 Flies and Half-Truths *(1976), 140cm × 120cm (4ft 8in × 3ft 11in); flat tapestry*

10.6

Kathleen McFarlane

NORFOLK

Kathleen McFarlane was born in Sunderland, the industrial north-east of England, in 1922. She trained and worked, uninspired, as a librarian during the dreary war years, then, in 1944 she married James McFarlane and they set up home in Oxford where he was reading for a degree in German. In a culturally more enlightened climate, life began to open up for her.

Three years later they moved back to the north for her husband to take up his first teaching post at the University of Newcastle-on-Tyne. Now she was more culturally aware and freer to consider what her right *métier* might be. She would have liked to study painting. Victor Pasmore was Master of Painting at Newcastle University and his work and precepts were at the centre of a whirlpool of creative thought and activity. However, she decided instead to join her husband in the study of the Norwegian language, a decision which was to prove of the utmost importance to them. It resulted in his total transference to the study of Scandinavian culture and literature and in particular to the study of Ibsen, on whom he is now a world authority. Kathleen became a proficient and valued translator, but her frequent stays in Norway had another result: she was taught to weave by an elderly Norwegian weaver. She acquired a loom and, using the sound Scandinavian textile skills of superb craftsmanship, natural yarns, subtle, natural colour and traditional complex patterns, kept her home and her growing family supplied with rugs, blankets, cushions, bags and all the other many textile needs.

For a while, her family, her translating and her practical weaving kept her occupied, but there was still a cultural need unfulfilled and she returned once more to the thought of painting. She attended painting and life-drawing classes as an occasional student and was much ener-

11.1

gized by being in the thick of Victor Pasmore's circle of influence. His rejection of figurative painting in favour of the study of basic form was very much to her liking: 'For me, it was a period of exploration, with no pressures and no compulsions but my own. I allowed myself to be influenced by whom I chose and felt my way untuitively through a ferment of ideas.' Other than Pasmore, the most important influences on her were the Norwegian painter Edvard Munch, Jean Arp, Baumeisler and Henry Moore. Moore's work had been the first to make her realize that both the practice and the contemplation of art is a deeply moving and spiritual experience. Her particular interest, when

11.1 *Kathleen McFarlane in her studio garden*

11.2 Black Fir *(1965), 60cm × 45cm (2ft × 1ft 6in); relief painting*

11.3 Primeval Forest *(1967), 107cm × 107cm (3ft 6in × 3ft 6in); painting*

11.4 Black Fungoid *(1969), 90cm × 130cm (3ft × 4ft 2in); wool tapestry*

11.5 Spring Mutation *(1972), 100cm × 140cm (3ft 3in × 4ft 6in); weaving and crochet in undyed sisal string*

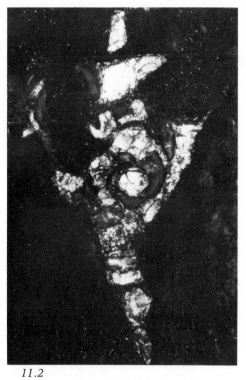

11.2

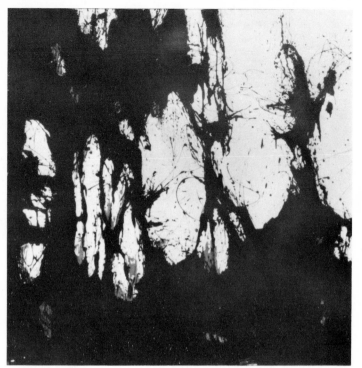

11.3

11.4

11.5

11.6

11.7

drawing and painting, came to be in the internal structure, patterns and organic nature of things.

In 1964 the family moved to Norwich for Professor McFarlane to take the chair of European Literature at East Anglia University. The local flints, so reminiscent of the forms of Arp and Henry Moore, proved a new and absorbing interest for her. Of interest too was the new world of visual experience opened up by the electron microscope, and she was riveted by the patterns of growth of living organisms and the effect of growth forces on structure. Her *Primeval Forest* was produced at this time (illustration 11.3). 'I have always worked intuitively, deliberately choosing not to seek to analyse or to explain what I do; as long as the ideas were coming I chose not to disturb them by too much reason.'

Living in Norwich rather than the north made London a little more accessible and thus the exhibitions. She became interested in the American Abstract Expressionists, Robert Motherwell, Clifford Still, Helen Frankenthaler and Adolph Gottlieb. 'They were creating bold and

powerful images that were full of mystery and strange symbolism for me.' Contemplating their work helped her use paint more freely and gave her the courage 'to venture into the unknown with the expectation of discovering something which I could not work out on the drawing board.' Other influences were Tapies, Burri, and Dubuffet, precisely because of their textural treatment of paint. Gradually, she began to experiment with materials like plaster, sand, sacking and foil, and produced *Black Fir* (illustration 11.2). Weaving had been a satisfactory method of producing domestic textile goods for a while but had slowly become a routine, and was thus dropped.

Then, beginning in 1967, a series of events happened which were to make everything 'come together'. First she saw an exhibition of Yugoslav tapestries from Novi Sad in the local art gallery. There they were, like huge, abstract, expressionist paintings, but glowing with the warm lustre of wool, and she realized that what she wanted to do was paint with wool. She discovered Tadek Beutlich's *Technique of Woven Tapestry* and proceeded to weave

86

11.8

in tapestry technique, instead of to paint, her interior images. *Black Fungoid* (illustration 11.4) was of this period and after an exhibition locally she was commissioned to weave an altar frontal for St Margaret's Priory, Kings Lynn. She says:

In my painting I had come to be pre-occupied with surface-texture. I went through the same process with tapestries, from weaving flat, two-dimensional pieces, I began to address myself to the creation of low reliefs and texture. The diversity of materials and techniques encouraged every sort of experimentation and I got carried away by them. I soon came to realize, however, that I had been seduced by the intrinsic beauty and fascination of the materials and that they did not fit the sort of images I wanted to create. The work tended to a sort of prettiness and decorativeness that was out of character.

The next happening was the final and most important of all – a catalyst. Visiting Amsterdam to look at Rembrandt paintings, she came upon the fibre-sculpture work of the great Polish artist-weaver, Magdalena Abakanowicz, in the Stedelijk Museum. This artist and her work were hitherto totally unknown to her. Also the work of Tadek Beutlich took her breath away and finally settled everything into place for her. This, she felt, was how things should be – powerful forms produced in powerful materials (sisal), more meaningful by far than anything else she had ever encountered.

They disturbed the recesses of my mind as nothing else since Henry Moore has done. Abakanowicz spoke in a new language but one I felt I readily understood. I began working in sisal instead of wool and it was a revelation. I succumbed totally to the new material

11.6 Poryfera I *(1973), 284cm × 195cm (9ft 5in × 6ft 4in); dyed sisal, weaving and crochet*

11.7 Black Tang *(1974), 240cm × 240cm (8ft × 8ft); dyed sisal, weaving, crochet and binding*

11.8 Golden Fungoid *(1975), 183cm × 183cm (6ft × 6ft); weaving and crochet*

and exulted in the results I could get from it. The greatest excitement in the early stages came from the forms I could make in sisal with the familiar crochet hook. Forms that seemed to grow under my hands as if obeying some inner law struck such a chord in me that my hands trembled as I worked. I had clearly stumbled on something which had a very profound meaning for me.

At last she had found the right medium for expressing herself and from then on worked with greater confidence and total conviction. *Spring Mutation* (illustration 11.5), for her a most important work, was exhibited – and to her surprise sold! More work sold, a token that others too saw the validity of what she was doing. Work grew larger, two large pieces, *Poryfera I* and *II* (illustration 11.6), were exhibited in the important 'Craftsman's Art' exhibition at the Victoria and Albert Museum, London. Norwich Castle Museum purchased one of these. Work poured out, exhibitions came thick and fast. She had a one-woman exhibition in Edinburgh. She acquired an upright frame-loom and this helped her to emerge into a new freedom. Works could be produced which could be totally three-dimensional, and could be viewed from all round. Of her work at this time, she writes:

The discovery of the power of sisal as a medium and the new potential of the large scaffold weaving frame, 300 × 270 cm (10ft × 9ft), combined to change in dramatic fashion the direction of my work. Sisal, with its marvellously organic qualities, adapted itself admirably to the forms and textures which had so preoccupied me in recent years. It proved to be so incredibly versatile: it came in a range of thicknesses and structures; it could be knotted, wrapped, or unravelled to form new and exciting textures; it not only lent itself to traditional weaves like soumak and twining, giving them new artistic dimensions, but it also opened up endless opportunities for invented techniques.

Simultaneously with this, the new technical freedom which the use of the frame loom made possible was accompanied by a new kind of creative freedom. The fact that the entire work could be seen as a developing whole – in contrast to the limited possibilities offered by the traditional loom where only a few inches could be seen at any one time – meant that it was no longer necessary to design the total work in detail in advance as previously, and instead a more spontaneous approach was made possible – the piece could be allowed to grow as an organic unity, to develop (at least in part) in obedience to its own innate compulsions as it took shape. For me, it is only when a dialectic of this kind begins to operate between myself and the work that things really start to happen. It is a process which is even more effective, I have discovered, in the manipulation of two-dimensional woven pieces into three-dimensional sculptural forms, where there are no established techniques or rules and you are left with only the intrinsic quality of the material and your own intuitions to guide you.

The technical problems to emerge from this way of weaving have been my principal concern in recent years. The difficulties are those of making an essentially pliable fabric or woven artefact hold a three-dimensional form. I dislike using armatures or other types of rigid supports in the body of a tapestry, partly on purist grounds, partly because of the complications that arise when transporting and mounting exhibitions (especially if I cannot be there to supervise the hanging). Nor are glues wholly satisfactory, especially in the case of heavy materials, though admittedly they are invaluable for securing knots and occasional reinforcings. Stuffing, on the other hand, has, where appropriate, much to commend it. But the most effective solution, I find, is to create a firm skeletal structure with stitching – several rows of firm overstitching can provide a good firm support and can moreover on suitable occasions be used on the visible parts of the work as part of the overall design.

From choice I would work on a large scale, as I believe my best work is in this area; but the problems not only of working alone without a battery of equipment but also of transporting and marketing such unwieldy objects are a considerable inhibition.

In 1976, at the British Crafts Centre in London, a one-woman show of her work put her very firmly and clearly in focus as the dynamic and complete artist she now is. The works were all three-dimensional, shaped, thrusting and vigorous. They occupied their positions in space with enormous presence and with no doubt of their power and purpose. All influences and techniques had been absorbed and extraneous matter had dropped away leaving the nucleus of her vision and strength. Particular works were *Black Tang* (illustration 11.7), *Golden Fungoid* (illustration 11.8) and *Red Totem* (illustration 11.9). Colours were rich, lustrous, glowing and positive.

Kathleen McFarlane has said, 'People often ask me what my work is about and this is difficult to answer. I can only say that my work is manifestations in concrete form of previously unformed images in my mind. I feel my way towards them rather than work from pre-formed ideas. They are very much a part of me and when they are complete, I feel they could not possibly be any different from the way they are. They are as familiar to me as my own children.'

Her early work was about organic growth, her latest work has a sexual impact but not in the accepted sense of the term. It links together sexual images with the cataclysm of birth, but in a cosmic way. It seems to be about the evolution of the universe, ever unfolding, erupting eternal. If Abakanowicz is creating forms to remind us of the need to keep in tune with our organic nature and natural rhythms, then Kathleen McFarlane is, in her present work, telling us about the nature of our explosive and dynamic universe.

11.9

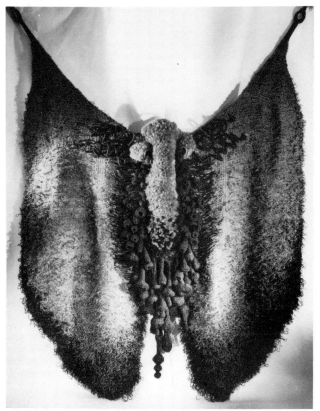

11.9 Red Totem *(1975), 214cm × 120cm (7ft × 4ft); weaving and crochet*

11.10 Le Rouge et Le Noir *(1976), 240cm × 366cm (8ft × 12ft); weaving, winding and crochet*

11.10

Theo Moorman, M.B.E.

PAINSWICK, GLOUCESTERSHIRE

Theo Moorman was born in 1907 in Leeds, Yorkshire, the textile industrial north of England, and came of an academic family.

At the age of 18 she embarked upon a three-year course at the Central School of Arts and Crafts in London, studying hand-weaving under the tutelage of Walter Taylor, who had been an apprentice of William Morris. At this place and time, the study of handweaving encompassed only three clearly defined aspects of the subject — dress or furnishing yardage, rugs and tapestry weaving. This was all treated in a very flat and two-dimensional manner, sober in colour, serious and confined in intent and very much a 'craft' in the medieval sense of the word. She still regrets the lack of drawing and painting content in the instruction at that point in her training.

Once out of college her first employment was to weave rugs in the craft workshops of the premises of Heal & Sons Ltd in Tottenham Court Road, London — a fine opportunity as Heal's was, in the 1930s, a spearhead of thinking in contemporary furnishings and fine craftsmanship. After two years she left Heal's to try her hand at freelance weaving from her London 'bed-sitter' — 'a bed-sitter full of loom' — but it was not long before she again found herself an employee, this time of Warner & Sons Ltd of Braintree in Essex. Originally silk weavers of Spitalfields, they were the makers of hand- and powerloom furnishing damasks, brocades and velvets of the finest quality, and their products were used for coronation robes and ceremonial regalia. Her job in the 1930s was to help create a new line of modern simple fabrics, the main design element of which would be the then-new textured yarns, often in the new manmade fibres — work much to her taste.

In 1939 the Second World War put an end to such matters and the next few years were spent helping develop highly tech-

12.1

nically specialized fabrics for use in the tools of war. This was a dark period for her as it was for everyone, but it added something to her skill in handling fine and closely-set yarns with great accuracy. It was ended three years later with the opportunity to work with the Council for the Encouragement of Music and the Arts, the forerunner of the Arts Council of Great Britain, back in her native Yorkshire, organizing art exhibitions and cultural happenings. The following nine years broadened her vision and deepened her aesthetic awareness, necessitating, as it did, a familiarization with the drawing, painting, sculpture, music, drama and theatre of the day.

In 1953 she felt the need to return to

12.1 *Theo Moorman* MBE

12.2 Tree Bark, *linen and cotton*

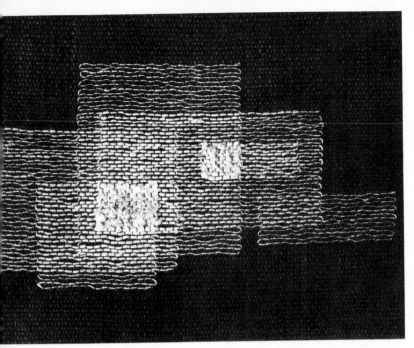

12.3

or painting and sculpture – she has been much influenced by the work of Henry Moore and the paintings of Ben Nicholson. Always there is flow and harmony – even in discord. She says, 'My desire is to express and communicate something of my response to my environment through my craft. I am concerned with producing woven abstractions from my visual experiences. These abstractions may deviate so far from the original literal image as to be unrecognizable but I hope that they retain much of the primary vision and impulse.' Many of her ideas see the first light of day as small hangings intended for a domestic setting, but most of her large works have been commissioned by the Church. She does not often use symbolism in an ecclesiastical sense, but incorporates a sense of flow and harmony which gives substance to feelings of peacefulness and unity. The weaving technique she uses (illustration 12.3) is one of free shuttling overshot weaving in fine yarns on lightweight, plain ground weaves, almost airy, translucent versions of tapestry. She almost invariably works in the finest of yarns, mostly 80/2 mercerized cottons and Swedish linens.

The technique was developed because she wanted to create her free graphic forms in a swifter manner than in the traditional tapestry technique. She writes 'It appeared that two things had to happen. Firstly, the inlaid areas of colour had to be bound down to the ground weave by a tie-down warp thread which was fine enough to be barely visible but strong enough to stand up to the strains to which it would be subjected. Secondly the cloth structure had to be designed so that the ground wefts, running from selvedge to selvedge, would lie at the back of the areas of inlay, somehow hidden away so that they would not break into the colour areas, but at the same time would form a solid cloth background.' A ground weave warp is entered on two shafts, the finer tie-down warp, which is every third thread, is entered on a further two shafts, and thus the tie-down threads can either be woven in with the ground cloth or be lifted independently to accommodate the surface free-shuttling. The technique is a very accurate one and no distortion of the horizontal path of the weft threads occurs.

weaving once more but this time in a very different and highly personal manner, with the handloom as a vehicle and tool for her own visual imagery. At first, and still located in Yorkshire, she worked with the help of the sculptor Austin Wright, interpreting his drawings through the medium of her fine weavings, and this ultimately resulted in commissions for work to be placed in Wakefield and Manchester cathedrals.

Finally, she decided to move south to the cottage in the village of Painswick in Gloucestershire where she now lives and works, and thus to embark upon the period of work in which all her earlier experiences and influences could come together. The work at first had an element of the bold and rugged in it such as is seen in the altar throw-over for Manchester, but has gradually refined and crystallized to a fine graphic airiness – subtle, low-key, with something of the lightness of Chinese art, paper and bamboo, using flat, often translucent, areas of weaving.

She is a totally dedicated artist-craftswoman of immense patience. She has no helpers, every inch of her work comes from her own hands. Her imagery is drawn from the stones, air, water, trees and light of her environment, sometimes from architecture

12.4

She herself says: 'Only the weaving I have produced in the last 10 or 15 years has any real merit or validity and this shows the serious waste of time that can result from an inability to think a problem out logically from the roots upwards rather than plunging in and only learning from the mistakes of impetuosity.' Her greatest strengths are subtlety of line, shape and colour, delicacy of vision and technique, refinement, superb craftsmanship and a unity of vision.

She manages to incorporate a degree of teaching and lecturing into her yearly schedule, generally in the United States, and is known for being an enthusiastic and generous teacher. In 1975 she wrote a book about her life and work called *Weaving as an Art Form, a Personal Statement*. In it she deals with her methods of weaving, and designing and executing work in detail, but to read it is to learn far more than about the art of weaving alone.

Recently new developments have come about in her work (illustration 12.7). They are still of the finest threads and of great delicacy but as she is fired by the work of the painter Richard Smith, they have become gently three-dimensional and have broken away from rectangular boundaries. She is exploring the effects of light and shade on different woven surfaces by inserting into a basic hanging separately woven, sometimes shaped, strips of weaving, inserting them by varied means into the ground so that they break out of a basic surface in many directions and planes. Sometimes the basic ground plane weft itself breaks away and becomes part of a tiny warp itself and for this work she often uses two looms, inserting the product of one into the product of the other. She says, 'As new techniques develop, the need becomes constantly more pressing to put them to the right use – the increasing aesthetic responsibility imposed by the enlargement of technical knowledge is something we ignore at our peril.'

In 1977, in the Jubilee and Birthday Honours List, Theo Moorman was awarded an MBE.

12.3 *Close-ups of the overlay technique which Theo Moorman uses in most of her works*

12.4 *Nave altar throw-over, Manchester Cathedral (1968); predominantly wools, cottons and linens in flames and silvers*

12.5

12.6

94

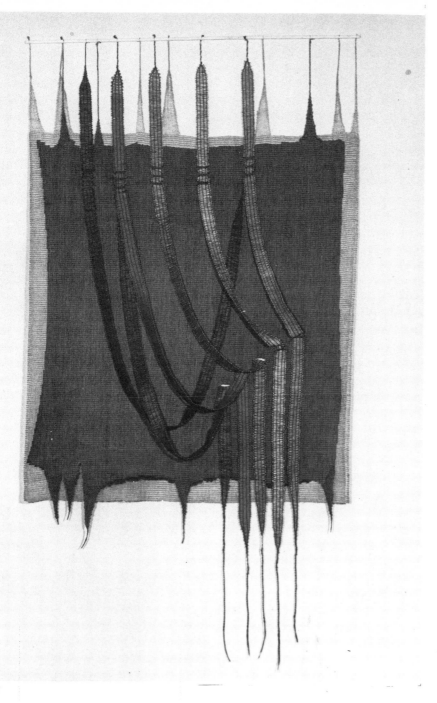

12.7

12.5 *Space dividers for Ashleworth Court,*
    Gloucestershire (1966); wool and linen

12.6 Manhatten *(1974), 140cm × 96cm*
    (4ft 8in × 3ft 2in); linen and cotton
    wallhanging

12.7 Orange and Pink *(1975), 65cm × 120cm*
    (2ft 4in × 4ft); linen and cotton
    wallhanging

Alec Pearson

CAMBRIDGE

Alec Pearson was born in Yorkshire in 1924. He received his art training as a painter at Keighley and Leeds Colleges of Art, and in Paris and Germany, a training interrupted and delayed by the war years. As a painter his main themes have always been based on landscape, which he sees with a lyrical mysticism. His main medium in recent years has been watercolour.

In 1947 he embarked upon an art teaching career, in both general and further education. He first taught at Accrington School of Art, in the north, then King Edward's Grammar School, Aston, in the industrial Midlands, and there became Head of Art at Sheldon Heath Comprehensive School, Birmingham. In 1962 he became a lecturer at Homerton College, Cambridge, and finally Head of Art at another college of education, the College of All Saints, London. During all this time he continued to draw, paint and exhibit.

Early in his career he had done a little tabby weaving on a table loom. He had an even earlier contact with wool, because his father was a 'colour matcher' in the woollen mill in the village – that is, he developed new shades and mixtures – and Alec Pearson was used to seeing his father experimenting with wool. This inborn sympathy for the material was later revived, partly through reading Tadek Beutlich's *The Technique of Woven Tapestry*, and he began to ask other weavers about types of looms and eventually bought a scaffold loom from Archie Brennan in Edinburgh. Around 1973 he wove a rug which seemed more valid as a wall-hanging. The new technique opened up for him the possibility of extending his pictorial ideas, on a larger scale, in the form of tapestries. So all-absorbed did he become in tapestry that at the end of 1974 he gave up full-time teaching in order to concentrate exclusively on the work of a tapestry and painting studio.

13.1

His watercolours are very small, yet his tapestries are fairly large, their average size being 1.5m × 1.2m (5ft × 4ft), and the largest to date 3.3m × 2.4m (11ft × 8ft). The two media are used to express the same root-interest in landscape, much of it in the English Lake District, where he spends a proportion of his time each year working out ideas. He rarely draws or paints on the spot, but tends to work indoors, selecting and developing forms and colours which seem important at the time. The results are representational in the sense that they are based on landscape.

When he starts a tapestry, the warp, double thickness linen at four ends per 2.5cm (1in), is set up by being wound continuously round top and bottom bars until the required width has been reached.

13.1 *Alec Pearson*

13.2 Islands on a Lake *(1976), 125cm × 150cm (4ft 2in × 5ft); wool on linen*

13.3 Mountains with Lake *(1975/6), 125cm × 150cm (4ft 2in × 5ft); wool on linen*

13.4 Tarns *(1975), 135cm × 110cm (4ft 6in × 3ft 8in); wool on linen (private collection, London)*

13.5 Black Fells *(1976), 150cm × 122cm (5ft × 4ft); wool on linen*

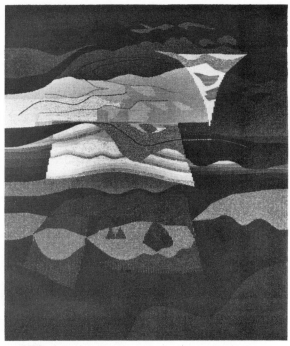

13.2

13.3

13.4

13.5

13.6

A drawing, a painting or a previous tapestry is the point of departure for the new work, and it is usual for him to make a full-size diagram in broad outline, which is fixed behind the warp. Once the weaving has got under way, progressing at about 30sq cm (1sq ft) each day, he begins to design freely, as he does in his drawings and paintings. The slow rate of weaving allows time for anticipating and changing. Often he draws with a felt pen onto the warp, making several versions of the solution to a problem. Out of the apparent confusion of lines the decision to weave a certain shape emerges. The process of weaving is thus never boring. He says that painting in textile fabric' is a fair description of his work. 'Painting and weaving do not imitate each other. The depth of colour in an area of weaving has an affinity with the depth of colour in a watercolour wash'. But this is as far as the analogy goes. Weaving is as free as painting, but each has its own possibilities and limitations.

After trying out methods of using leashes and rods he decided that finger-shedding (that is, raising the warp ends in the right order with the fingers) was the quickest and easiest way for him. It is quiet and uncomplicated and it means that every millimetre of both warp and weft runs through his fingers giving him control over tension. Although he attached great importance to perfecting this simple technique he is more concerned with imagery than with technical innovations. He dyes

13.6 Mountain and Lakes *in production*

13.7 Mountain and Lakes *(1976), 165cm × 122cm (5ft 6in × 4ft); wool on linen (collection of Arthur Anderson & Co., London)*

13.8 Brown Tarn *(1975), 113cm × 136cm (3ft 2in × 4ft 6in); wool on linen (collection of Arthur Anderson & Co., London)*

13.9 Pink Tarns *(1976/7) 122cm × 91cm (4ft × 3ft); wool on linen (private collection)*

13.10 Tarn *(1975), 150cm × 122cm (5ft × 4ft); wool on linen (collection of Joshua Taylor & Co., Cambridge)*

98

13.7

13.8

13.9

13.10

13.12

white, grey and natural black yarns with a rull range of colours using commercial dyes.

He exhibits regularly, and in his comparatively short and new career as a tapestry weaver has already executed some large and important commissions. In the work of Alec Pearson we are absorbed into a world of mountain, tree, water, sky, reflection and atmosphere, which is rich and ambiguous and which allows us too to give rein to our imagination. There is no need at the moment for his technique to vary, as it so perfectly gives substance to his particular vision.

13.11 *Two tapestries commissioned for the foyer of the Guildhall School of Music, Barbican, London, with the support of the Radcliffe Trust and the Worshipful Company of Dyers*

13.12 *One of the two tapestries at the Guildhall School of Music, Barbican, London (1977), 240cm × 330cm (8ft × 11ft); wool on linen*

Maggie Riegler

ABERDEENSHIRE

Maggie Riegler happened to be born in Darjeeling, India, in 1944 but all her roots are Scottish. When she was six her parents, who remained in India, sent her back to Scotland to be educated in Aberdeen. It was there that she later received her art training, at Grays School of Art. For the first two years of this training, from 1962 onwards, she studied painting but the course was too academic for her tastes and she came to the conclusion that she could develop more fully by means of the crafts, particularly printed, embroidered and woven textiles which she studied for a further two years.

During these studies she had visited North Africa where the homogeneity of the local traditional weaving to its surroundings seemed a valid object-lesson. At the end of her studies she was awarded a post-graduate scholarship with which she studied in Europe and Scandinavia, particularly Finland where she found herself fascinated by the bold painterly textiles being produced in the Marimekko studios at Helsinki.

In 1966 she was appointed lecturer in weaving and embroidery at Grays, where she was to remain for eight years, meanwhile marrying Stewart Johnston, the potter. During this time her method of expressing herself through the medium of weaving and its allied techniques became more and more fluid. It is nature which is her springboard and impetus. She writes, 'When ideas become dislocated it is nature which provides the link. To see how a gnarled tree-bole can accommodate smooth young twigs, moss and an elephant-like fungus all in one area is to be given a lesson in the perfect assembly of incongruous elements. It is not my aim to copy nature faithfully – pointless, for how to begin to reproduce the perfection of a birch tree in form and function; and if such a facsimile of form were achieved it would

14.1

be a proof only of ingenuity not artistry.' She translates what she sees into textile objects which are sometimes flat, sometimes three-dimensional, always shaped. The objects are full of impact, strong, impelling, colourful, decorative, exotic.

Her inherited traits and her successive environments have all played their part in her development. Her family grounding is in the villages, birchwoods and moorlands of the valley of the River Dee in the

14.1 *Maggie Riegler at the loom*

14.2 Palm Tree *(1973), 180cm × 60cm (6ft × 2ft); tapestry, macramé, wrapping and plaiting*

102

north-east of Scotland; her early child-hood in India endowed her with a strong, warm colour and pattern sense and that early introduction to the brilliant has been deepened and softened by a return to the Scottish ambience.

Because she set out to be a painter she is concerned with the core of things but she had soon recognized that it was more relevant for her to draw with yarns, feathers and fabrics than with the brush or pencil. Sketches or drawings for works are minimal, the ideas are worked out directly into the materials in an immediate manner. The objects are vibrantly textural and have been described as capable of conveying as much to a blind person as to a sighted one. Like nature, surface areas are of infinite variegation and every part makes its own particular, individual, visual and textural statement.

The growth of *Roots* (illustration 14.7) from a mental embryo to a finished piece illustrates the process. The idea was to achieve something totally organic, with no hard rectangular edges, a growing thing. Therefore a conventional tapestry would be irrelevant – the thing must be shaped, textured, contoured. Three separate warps were set up side by side so that each piece of weaving could be shaped in relation to the others. It became obvious as the pieces progressed that robust texture was necessary; heaviness, strength and underground sombreness were what she wanted, so gradually thick knots of black cotton were introduced into the surface, gradually softening to charcoal greys and browns as the root system reached an imaginary earth-crust. When the weaving was completed and cut off the loom, she bunched the warps together at both ends to help continue the idea of natural growth – large chunks at the top, thick wraps to suggest the tree above, thinning off to fine tendrils and root wisps below.

Her interest has never centred on any particular textile technique exclusively. The techniques she uses are the immediate answer to a particular and urgent need – whatever is right for the inter-pretation on hand at the moment – winding, wrapping, simple weave techniques, stitch-ing, stuffing, knotting – 'the simpler the tools and the construction, the easier it is for the artist to impose his own ideas on

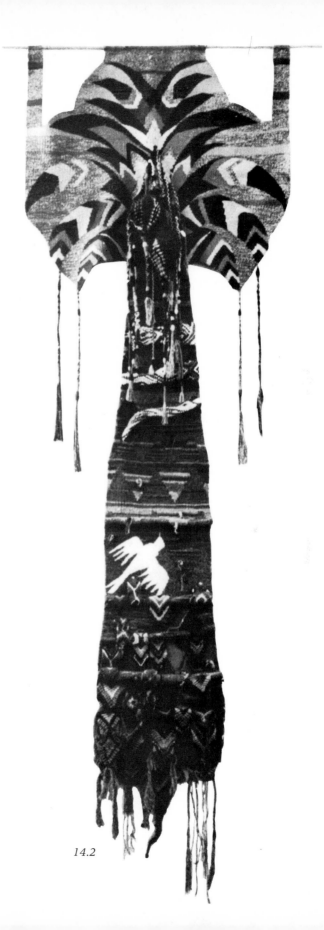

14.2

14.3

14.3 Midnight Moth *(1973), 150cm × 125cm*
(5ft × 4ft 2in); tapestry weave and
macramé knotting (collection of the Royal
Scottish Museum, Edinburgh)

14.4 Bird *(1972), 180cm × 45cm (6ft × 1ft 6in);*
wrapping, plaiting, macramé; cotton,
wool, camel-hair, goat-hair, silk (private
collection)

14.5 *Detail of* Bird

14.6 Dickon's Bonfire *(1976), 25cm × 37cm*
(10in × 15in); miniature; tapestry weave
and wrapping

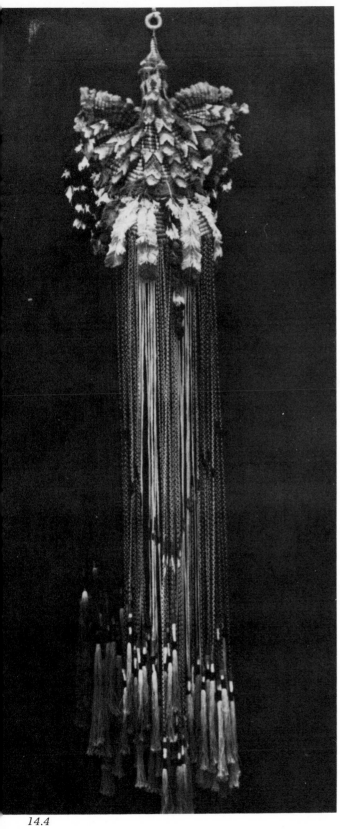

14.4

14.5

14.6

14.7

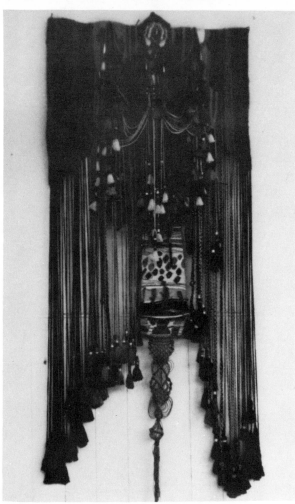

14.8

the object, to break the rhythm and introduce new elements, to produce a personal statement'. Often the component textile parts are each treated as yet further raw materials and in their turn folded, three-dimensionalized, stitched and formed. There is a building up and an adding on of complex components into the cohesive whole. In general her works are of 'average' size but she equally enjoys working small (illustration 14.6) and large (illustration 14.8), though the latter poses some difficult practical problems. Her present work area is a corner of the living-room where she can easily keep an eye on her children. She does not consider this entirely as a disadvantage and half-quotes Dr Johnson (who was speaking of the prospect of death) when she says 'The imminent thunder of tiny feet concentrates the mind wonderfully.'

She considers Raoul d'Harcourt's *Textiles of Ancient Peru and their Techniques* a particularly inspiring book and finds within it that which she most admires, 'a combination of artistry, craftsmanship and ingenuity'.

Of her work *in toto* and her methods of working she says,

> I feel an underlying continuum in every-thing that is done, that each piece finished, however far it is from my original goal, has added some tiny fragment of knowledge, either visual or technical. The goal is to try to achieve something, a fraction, of the perfection I see every day in nature; a sense of organic growth, of wholeness, of begin-ning and ending naturally. The goal of achieving something that just *is* without 'cleverness' or *trompe l'oeil*, an object where the technique is totally sub-ordinated to the idea.

14.7 *Detail of* Boudoir Bat

14.8 Boudoir Bat *(1974), 225cm × 105cm (7ft 6in × 3ft 6in); tapestry, knotting, plaiting, tasselling, wrapping (collection of the Scottish Arts Council)*

14.9 *Hanging (1968)*

106

14.10

14.11

14.10 Eden Court Tapestry *(1977) 210cm ×
570cm (7ft × 19ft); mural commissioned
for the Eden Court Theatre, Inverness*
14.12 *Detail of* Eden Court Tapestry

14.11 *Detail of* Roots *(1974), 147cm × 80cm
(4ft 7in × 2ft 8in); tapestry stuffed and
contoured (private collection)*

14.12

Sax Shaw

EDINBURGH

Sax Shaw was born in Huddersfield in 1916. Between 1936 and 1938 he studied at Huddersfield School of Art, going on from there to Edinburgh College of Art to work in stained glass. The war intervened. After the war he returned to Edinburgh to take a post-graduate course in stained glass, mosaic and mural design, at the end of which he was awarded an Andrew Grant travel scholarship. He used the scholarship to travel to France where, at the Musée des Arts Decoratifs in Paris, he encountered an exhibition of the great new modern French tapestries, the design and production of which had been revitalized by the work of Lurçat, Saen-Saens, Dom-Robert and other artists. Immensely impressed by the tapestries and the medium of wool and the weaving technique, he took himself to the Gobelin works in Paris where, in particular, he saw some small tapestries in production which had within them areas of texture of particular subtlety and interest which he felt he wanted to emulate. It was while exploring the Gobelins that he encountered a dyer who said to him: 'Hold wool in your hands and then think with your heart' – a phrase which has remained in his mind ever since.

In Edinburgh, he was asked to join the staff of the College of Art to teach stained glass and architecture and this he has done ever since. He had, of course, after his discovery of the French tapestries, soon become aware of the Edinburgh Tapestry Company and from 1955 to 1960, in addition to his teaching, he was principal artist to the Company. The Company had been started in 1910 by the 4th Marquis of Bute, staffed by two master-weavers from the William Morris Studio, Merton Abbey, and later their apprentices. Its original function was the design and production of historical tapestry panels for the Marquis' home at Mount Stuart, Isle of Bute. In 1954 new directors took over from the

15.1

Bute family and decided that a more contemporary thinking was required. Shaw's first pieces of work for the Company were three tapestry panels for Lord Colum Chrighton-Stuart and these were followed by three stained-glass windows. During the five years that he was designer and also the Director of Weaving with the Company, he did indeed revolutionize its image, its thinking, and its methods of working. It was during this period that *Theseus and the Minotaur* (illustration 15.6) was produced.

Shaw is a man who has managed to live close to the mainstream of his existence, a man essentially at one with himself, his aims and his media, glass, wool and metal. Of these media he says, 'Stained glass and wool are alike – both alive with translucent light.' For his tapestries he produces preliminary paintings, often in watercolour, but while painting he is thinking in wool. Of his inspiration at any given time he says, 'An artist should be a sponge of the society in which he lives, soaking it up and telling us what it is like to be a man in his time.' In the late 1950s, under the influence of Lurçat, Shaw's work was

15.2

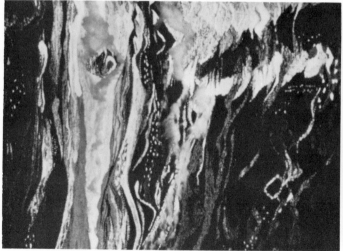

15.3

15.4

15.1 *Sax Shaw*

15.2 Carmargue *(1975), 101cm × 381cm
(3ft 4in × 12ft 6in), (commissioned by
Liverpool University Veterinary College)*

15.3 Raku *(1967), 109cm × 144cm (3ft 7in ×
4ft 8in), tapestry, cotton warp, spun
cheviot, lurex and fleece weft*

15.4 Re-entry *(1969), 270cm × 195cm
(9ft × 6ft 6in), (property of Salverson's,
Edinburgh)*

111

15.5

15.6

15.7

'semi-religious, semi-pagan'. In the 1960s he began to be much influenced by the ambience of the Carmargue area of France where he has spent much time (illustration 15.2). Then came *Raku*, stemming from a particular ceramic pot (illustration 15.3) but introducing an important new element, loose fibre, and *Re-entry* (illustration 15.4), the space-travel origins of which are obvious. Much of his work has been for the Church and much specially commissioned pieces by discerning private patrons, many in the USA.

In 1967 the American architect, Henry Hill, commissioned him to weave *Sea Cave* (illustration 15.5) for Jack Lund's home in San Francisco. The interior was designed around the tapestry. In 1968 he wove *Earth* (colour plate 6) for Leo Rothschild's home on the Solent in the south of England, and for the same client *Fire Tiger* (illustration 15.7). St Kentigern's Church, Edinburgh, to name but one out of many, is a testament to the versatility of his skills, containing as it does his tapestries, windows and metalwork.

Of his work Sax Shaw says:

My attitude is one of seeking a solution to problems posed by the materials and by discovering the intentions of my own mind. This approach is possible only in panels woven and designed by the same person and is filled with danger and delight. In this method the resultant panel is complete in design only when removed from the loom. It owes its existence to the ideas conveyed in the material and should be free of imposed pattern. Often the result produces a woven fabric which could never have been conceived in any paint or other medium beforehand. It is rich in wool colours and has a fascinating surface texture, only possible in weaving.

15.5 Sea Cave *(1967), 140cm × 150cm (4ft 6in × 5ft), (collection of Jack Lund, San Francisco)*

15.6 Theseus and the Minotaur *(1956), 132cm × 167cm (4ft 6in × 5ft 6in), (collection of Mark Norman)*

15.7 Fire Tiger *(1968), 121cm × 167cm (4ft × 5ft 6in), (Leo Rothschild Collection)*

Unn Sönju

LEEDS

Unn Sönju was born in Oslo, Norway, in 1938. She came to England when young and ever since has divided her time between the two countries. Between 1957 and 1959 she attended Leeds College of Art doing intermediate studies under such people as Harry Thubron, Terry Frost and Tom Hudson. It was a moment of great change in British art education and thus there was an air of high-level energy, discussion and ideas around. These years were informative and enlightening for her to an enormous degree.

In 1959 she decided to specialize in printed textiles, having come to the conclusion that she was not 'good enough' to be a fine artist. She enrolled at the Kolnishewerkschule in Cologne but the course did not satisfy her so she returned to her native Norway and there set up her own studio to produce printed textiles and appliqué embroideries and managed to 'make a small dent' in the Norwegian craft market. Of this period she writes,

> One day while I was printing and listening to the radio I heard a strange interview with a woman with a beautiful voice yet a very odd accent. The interviewer was asking about her vegetable dyes. To my delight this forthright and lovely lady described how she made her beautiful blue colours with her own urine. One could sense Norwegian radio turning bright red when she said 'Pissblue!' With the interview over I learned that this magnificent lady was the legendary poetess and 'picture weaver' Hannah Ryggen. This woman fired my imagination so much that I went straight back to college.

She enrolled at the Kvinnelige Industriskole in Oslo and spent a rigorous but rewarding two years learning all aspects of tapestry weaving. She knew now that she had found her right medium, and she says,

16.1

'In weaving, the artist and the medium enjoin in a symbiotic relationship.' She stresses however that it took much work, time, experimentation and questioning to reach any kind of understanding or conclusion.

In 1962 she married the British painter Miles McAlinden and settled in Leeds where he now teaches at the newly-named School of Creative Arts and Design, Leeds Polytechnic. In 1965 she was asked to set up, with Mary Auty, an experimental textile area within the Fine Art Department of the Polytechnic. The philosophy of the department was one of an open-ended enquiry into all aspects of visual art – a situation where student activities ranged from film to sculpture, performance to printing, ceramics to sound, writing to painting. The textile unit participated in this intermedia programme making costumes, sets, soft sculpture, printing and weaving of many persuasions. She lectures there still.

16.1 *Unn Sönju*

16.2 Styrstav (Balancing Rod) *(1974), 215cm × 150cm (7ft 2in × 5ft), half of a diptych*

114

16.2

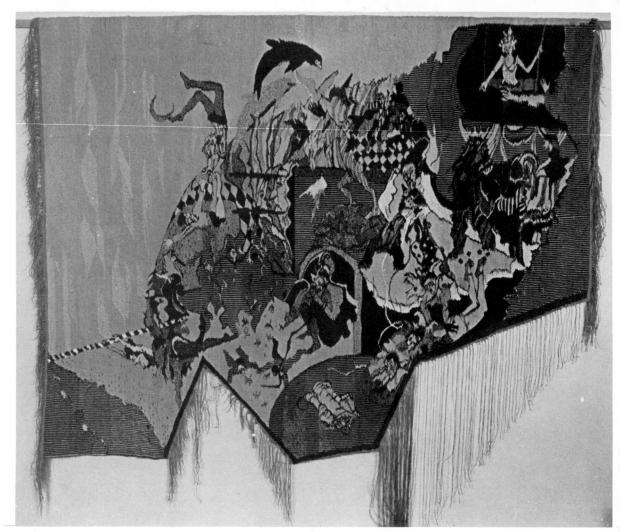

16.3

Unn Sönju's output of tapestry is prodigious, and it is exhibited in both Britain and Norway. In Britain it is often said that her work shows strong relationships with Nordic mythology and in Norway that it is strongly influenced by British contemporary art and surrealism. It may be true to say that she is slightly better known in Norway than Britain, largely due to Norway's unquestioning acceptance of the weaver as artist. She says that her attitudes have changed greatly since she started to weave. Her drawing and weaving were once quite separate and now they have become one. The tapestries contain figurative work and elements also of memory and dream and ambiguity.

Her drawings were already of an advanced standard when her first weavings were still 'hit and miss and undisciplined', but through constant work and experiment, the strong and vigorous imaginative vision apparent in her drawings has found even greater impact and freedom when translated into wool and tapestry weave and the 'akle' technique (a traditional rectilinear Norwegian technique). Everything is completed on the loom, there is no sewing up of vertical slits afterwards; in

16.3 Circus *(1976), 200cm × 250cm (6ft 6in × 8ft 4in); black, white, dark crimson, yellow (property of Stavanger Faste Galleri)*

16.4 *Detail of* Circus

16.5

fact she avoids the vertical and the horizontal. Sometimes she weaves the image sideways, sometimes upside down, thereby using the loom and the warp to her own advantage, and in general working in a manner which feels right for her drawings and the material. Of her work she says,

> I search to find a visual way to say the non-verbal, it is an adding-up process which sometimes leads to a surprising total. I am concerned with developing a strong visual language, compelling images and an addition to the vocabulary of art. As long ago as I can remember I have been drawing. The drawings have never been an imitation or even a recreation of reality. Although my work is figurative, it is very concerned with structure, surface and pictorial devices. The figuration is necessary for me to develop my work into richer areas of concern. Many elements in my tapestries deal with the force and vitality of fibres and wool structure, yet I restrict this to the flat as I find that the two-dimensional surface has more latitude in allowing many things to exist there, whereas three-dimensional structures have the same limitations as we find in our reality. Three-dimensional woven structures appear, like much contemporary sculpture, seemingly unable to equate figurative imagery in their totality. Their subject is their total non-figurative form – as is their object. I have always found this a restrictive limitation and feel that many weavers rely too much upon the surface and texture of their objects than on the total form and image power. In the surfaces of my tapestries I attempt to bring authority

16.6

16.7

and tension by mingling the drawing and structuring of the media. I strive to create an ambiguity of vision, so that as one reads the images they ebb and flow as one changes the centre of focus. I always feel that the identity of the idea is more important than materials or media. I am concerned with art and not too involved with craft, one must know the media but the media must never rule.

16.5 My Memories are like Torn Sheets *(1976), 155cm × 204cm (5ft 2in × 7ft 10in); black, white, blues, yellows, pink, red*

16.6 *Half of the diptych* Sturstav (Balancing Rod) *(1974), 215cm × 150cm (7ft 2in × 5ft)*

16.7 Utflukt (Excursion) *(1973), 168cm × 107cm (5ft 6in × 3ft 6in)*

Ann Sutton

DORSET

Ann Sutton was born in 1935 near Stoke-on-Trent, the 'Potteries' area of the Midlands, but though coming of a family connected with ceramics, clay was not the medium for her. It was a medium too malleable, too ready to have the craftsman's will imposed upon it – and too messy! Instead she sought a 'countable' medium which had an element of mathematical logic and which would have strong technical limitations within which one could work and against which one could push. What could answer such a need better than constructed textiles? Textile-making for her 'is a way of exploring a construction within the boundaries of a system'.

Between 1951 and 1955 she studied for her National Diploma in Design in Embroidery and Weaving at Cardiff College of Art. Weaving she found was her medium; embroidery proved to have too few limitations.

For the first years of her professional career she was very much involved in education, teaching weaving at the West Sussex College of Art, Worthing, for eight years and at Croydon College of Art for two. During this time she was, from 1958,

17.1

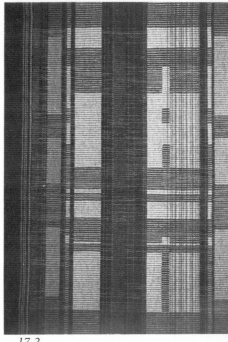

17.1 *Ann Sutton*

17.2 Atlantis *(1958), 140cm × 110cm (4ft 6in × 3ft 6in); a shaft-controlled warp repp hanging in blues, greens and black (collection of the Crafts Council of Great Britain)*

17.3 Pendant 1½ *(1966), 35cm × 9cm × 8cm (14in × 3½in × 3¼in); cotton, plain weave: in places woven as a double cloth; wood blocks inserted*

17.4 Pendant 3 *(1966), 9cm × 73cm × 8cm (3½in × 29in × 3¼in); cotton, plain weave: in places woven as a double cloth; wood blocks inserted (collection Victoria and Albert Museum)*

17.2

17.3

17.4

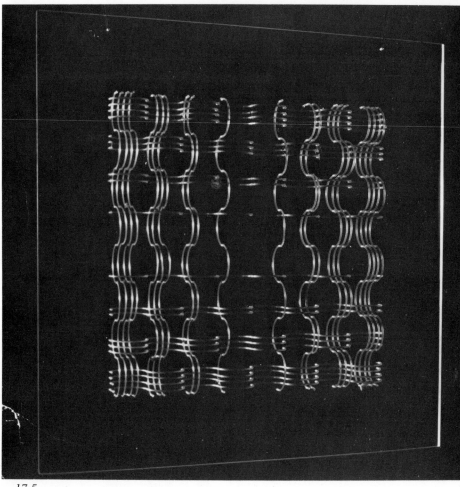

17.5

concerned with designing fabric as yardage and also as wallhangings, which were then a new concept in Britain. She received the Cotton Board's award for a woven fabric in 1962 and for a printed fabric (the first she had designed) in 1964. The wallhangings were very much loom-controlled (illustration 17.2) and often composed of new yarns like nylon monofilament.

In 1964 she married John Makepeace, a furniture designer and maker of international reputation. Together they set up their studios at Farnborough Barn in Oxfordshire. This was originally a corn barn set in open countryside which they renovated and extended until the whole was a satisfying arrangement of warm brick, natural wood and large areas of glass.

Her work had by now widened in its scope. Her ability to handle colour with authority led to a redesigned and recoloured range of traditional Welsh 'tapestry' (more correctly termed double cloth) bed covers suitable for the contemporary interior, and the 'cottage industry' production of knitted and crocheted mohair cushions. In the creation of wall- and spacehangings she began to incorporate wood blocks or mirror into plain weaves of fine cotton (illustration 17.3).

In 1967 she spent a very short period working with the sculptor Kenneth Martin, a period which she considers significant and which brought about a confirmation of her thoughts and feelings about the deep importance to her of the systems and logic inherent in the constructed textile medium.

In 1969 an exhibition of her work was held at the British Crafts Centre, London (illustration 17.6), where her interest in the textile structure as a sculptural three-

dimensional concept was made apparent in perspex panels, pierced and threaded with nylon monofilament (illustration 17.5) and in the knitted tubes forming space-hangings and light fittings. The knitted tubes were produced on hosiery knitting-machines. Also apparent was a concern with the graphic imagery emanating from thread and transparent fabric. These resulted in *Textile Images*, a collection of 16 textile image prints purchased and circulated by the Victoria and Albert Museum. *Bristle Box* (illustration 17.7) received an award from the Welsh Arts Council in their 'Sculpture 70' competition. In 1971 she was given a travel scholarship by the Royal Society of Arts and visited Morocco and Nigeria to study the application of two-dimensional pattern to three-dimensional forms and related this to the carpet designing with which she was then in-

volved. She was later elected a Fellow of the Royal Society of Arts.

In 1974 she moved her textile studio from Farnborough Barn itself to a chapel in the nearby village of Mollington, employing local, part-time workers, none of whom had had textile training. She is interested mostly in the initial concept of a design, and is willing to hand over the practical execution to competent workers who can be relied upon to produce work of technical excellence and craftsmanship. She quite enjoys the concepts engendered by

17.5 Invisible Weave *(1969), 30cm × 30cm (1ft × 1ft); acrylic panel, threaded with nylon monofilament*

17.6 *General view of one-man exhibition at the British Crafts Centre, London, 1969*

123

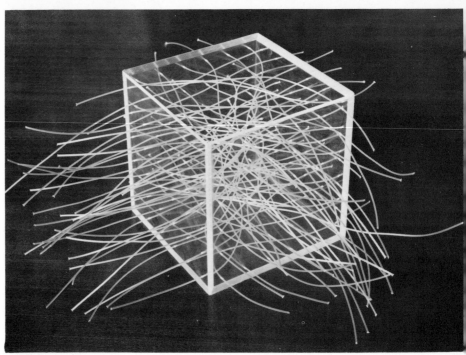

17.7

the fact that there is a piece of her work, in Britain, which she has never touched and never seen.

Ann Sutton has become absorbed by the unit and the module and the building up of these basic units into wholes which, though constructed of the same basic units as each other, vary totally in final character. This line of thought is underpinned by ever-constant fascination with the logic of numbers and numerical systems. She has said, 'Taking a simple unit, I apply the rules of a numerical discipline to it and sit back to watch the result. When construction-disciplines and numerical-disciplines unite, bells ring', and 'Numbers are vital contributors to each piece of work. . . . In most pieces a strict system of rules is adhered to in the making process and new techniques of textile making have to be volved. I work with invented structures; this involves much searching and many trials.' The units she uses are varied in technique but knitting and weaving are generally the bases, both for the unit itself and for the construction of the total object. One unit is the simple ring; it may be a ring of bunched threads or a ring of stuffed knitted tube; it may link with its fellows like a chain or like a doubled loop (illus-

trations 17.8 and 17.9). Another unit is the flat square, plain-woven either from thick threads or bunches of threads or from the stuffed knitted tube, or embellished with (long-pile) rya technique and produced on a nailed board. These are placed together to form rugs, wall and floor coverings, floor-pads and seating, and sometimes the floor, seat, and wall all in one.

A huge woven, knitted-tube floor pad, like a trampoline, was featured in the 'Craftsman's Art' Exhibition at the Victoria and Albert Museum in 1973 and later Liberty's commissioned a 'love-seat'. Finding an element such as the knitted tube, which she was able not only to stuff but also to join invisibly to itself, was very exciting.

Though they never physically work together, the creations of John Makepeace and Ann Sutton seem to have elements in

17.7 Bristle Box *(1970), maquette 30cm × 30cm × 30cm (1ft × 1ft × 1ft) for award winning sculpture, Welsh Arts Council*

17.8 Jacob's Florentine *(1976), 152cm × 152cm (5ft × 5ft), (collection of the artist)*

17.9 *Detail of* Jacob's Florentine

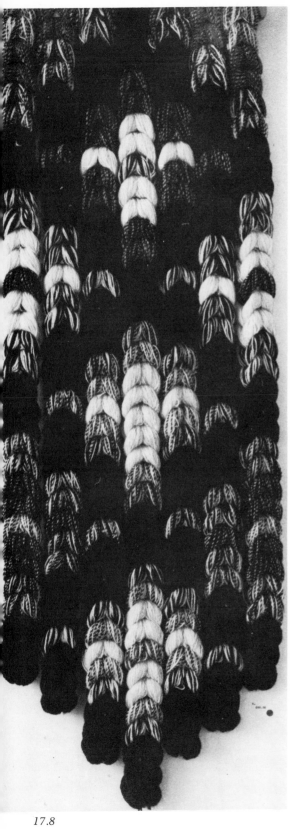

17.8

17.9

17.10

common. Just as he uses fine, superbly grained woods almost like textiles, so she builds her textile constructions into furniture-like objects (like the armchair in illustration 17.11).

After leaving Croydon, her teaching commitments were much reduced, being mainly in two centres: Banbury School of Art, where she was concerned with introducing first-year students to the possibilities of textiles, and Barry, South Wales, where she conducted summer schools. In 1975, in conjunction with Pat Holtom, she wrote *Tablet Weaving*, and participated in the creation of the International Exhibition of Miniature Textiles at the British Crafts Centre, London. In 1975 she had a second exhibition at the Crafts Centre. In 1976 she chaired the Fibre programme at the World's Crafts Council's General Assembly in Mexico.

In 1976 John Makepeace and Ann Sutton left Farnborough Barn for a larger establishment where they could extend their activities and where John could operate a two-year course for students in cabinet-making and furniture design. They are now established in Parnham House, a large, beautiful manor in Dorset, dating from 1470.

Ann Sutton's latest works are developing into larger, lighter-weight, airy pieces. Solidity is giving way to partial transparency and floating colour; they are still built up of units and implicit in them is always the logic of numbers. Many weavers are fascinated by the possibility of a square cloth with selvedge on all four sides, and her solution to this is used as a unit in these pieces in both visible and invisible form. Small squares of plain weaving, in yarns as different as mohair and nylon monofilament, are made upon nailed boards and then joined together.

Concerning her methods of working, Ann Sutton says 'I am concerned to demystify the textile technique cult, and have consciously eliminated loom-weaving from my work. Anything woven on a loom tends to be viewed with uncritical awe; observing that a piece is 'knitted' or 'darned' (techniques available to anybody), the viewer may be able to break through the mystique-technique barrier.'

She continues her 'cottage industry' line of activity and is increasingly interested in the development of craft industry in textile-making, in forms which enable the handweaver to obtain true recompense for his skill and craftsmanship. She is a textile innovator, a forward thinker in matters textile, and enjoys 'making things happen' whether in her studio or on the wider textile scene.

126

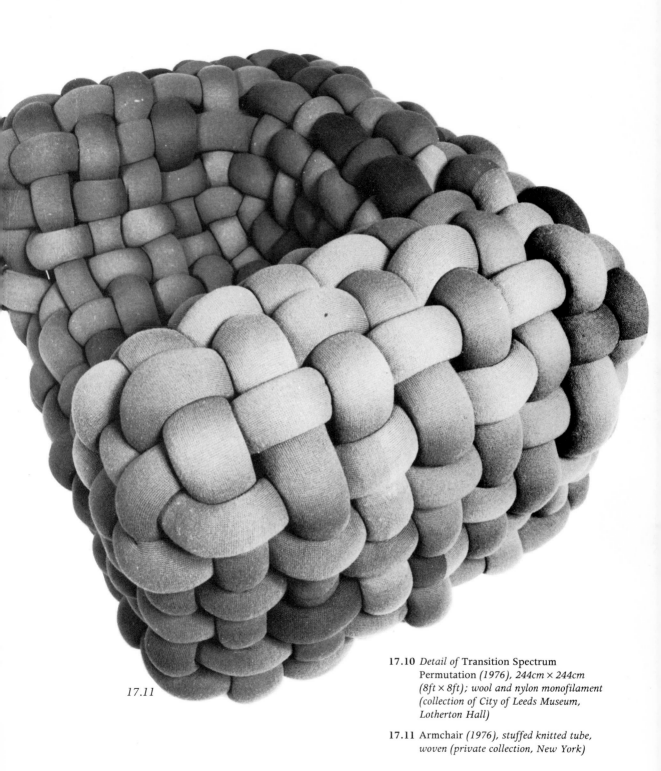

17.11

17.10 *Detail of* Transition Spectrum
Permutation *(1976), 244cm × 244cm
(8ft × 8ft); wool and nylon monofilament
(collection of City of Leeds Museum,
Lotherton Hall)*

17.11 Armchair *(1976), stuffed knitted tube,
woven (private collection, New York)*

127

Studio Addresses, Exhibitions, Commissions and Collections

Tadek Beutlich
Las Golondrinas, Camino de los Garcias, La Fustera, Benisa, Alicante, Spain

ONE-MAN EXHIBITIONS
1963, 1967, 1969, 1972 Grabowski Gallery.
1971–3 Croneen Gallery in Sydney and Melbourne, Australia.

GROUP EXHIBITIONS

1962, 1965, 1968 Xylon III, IV, V. International Exhibition of Woodcuts, Geneva, Switzerland.
1967 & 1969 3rd and 4th Biennale Internationale de la Tapisserie, Lausanne, Switzerland.
1969 Triennale Internazionale della Xilografia Contemporanea, Capri, Italy.
1970 International Print Biennale, Krakow, Poland.
1970–1 'British Designer Craftsmen', Smithsonian Institution, Washington DC.
1971 International Design Center, Minneapolis, USA.
1971 'Modern British Hangings', Scottish Arts Council, Edinburgh.
1971–2 'Deliberate Entanglements' Travelling Exhibition, Los Angeles, Vancouver, Chicago, etc.
1972 'Fibre Structures', The Denver Art Museum, USA.
1972 British International Print Biennial, Bradford, England.
1973 Victoria and Albert Museum, London.
1974 1st International Exhibition of Miniature Textiles, London.
1976 2nd International Exhibition of Miniature Textiles, London.

Archie Brennan
Edinburgh Tapestry Studios, Dovecot Road, Edinburgh, Scotland.

ONE-MAN EXHIBITIONS
1962 Tapestries Archie Brennan (Paperback Bookshop, Edinburgh).
1972 Archie Brennan, Tapestry, Scottish Arts Council Touring Exhibition.
1973 Muhammad Ali, 57 Gallery, Edinburgh.
1974 Muhammad Ali, City Art Gallery, Aberdeen.
1976 Archie Brennan, Tapestries, British Craft Centre.
1976 Narek Gallery, Canberra, Australia.
1976 Gryphon Gallery, Melbourne, Australia.

GROUP EXHIBITIONS
1962 Scottish Committee of the Arts Council of Great Britain, 'Jubilee of the Dovecot Tapestries 1912–1962'.
1963 Exhibition of Tapestry, Laing Gallery, Bradford.
'Experimental Tapestries by Scottish Weavers', Institute of Advanced Architectural Studies, University of York.
Exhibition of Tapestry, Art Gallery and Museum, Keighley.
1963–4 Travelling Exhibition of Tapestries, Victoria and Albert Museum, London.

1964 Exhibition at College of Further Education, Gloucester.
1965 'Weavers from the Dovecot Studios, Edinburgh', Whitworth Art Gallery, Manchester.
'Decorative Objects', Bear Lane Gallery, Oxford.
2nd Biennale Internationale de la Tapisserie, Lausanne.
1966 'Tapestries from the Dovecot Studios, Edinburgh', Laing Gallery, Bradford and the Art Gallery and Museum, Keighley.
Society of Scottish Artists Annual Exhibition.
1967 Society of Scottish Artists Annual Exhibition.
Spring Exhibition, City Art Gallery and Museum, Bradford.
1967 'Tapestries from the Dovecot Studios, Edinburgh', Institute of Advanced Architectural Studies, University of York.
1968 Society of Scottish Artists Annual Exhibition.
International Tapestry Exhibition, Prague.
1969 Society of Scottish Artists Annual Exhibition.
'Tapestry and Ceramics Today', English Speaking Union Gallery, Edinburgh.
'Legacy of Scotland', Hammond Museum, North Salem, New York.
'Church Embroidery and Handweaving of Today', York Minster.
1970 'Dovecot Tapestries', Scott-Hay Gallery, Langholm.
1970–1 'Modern British Hangings', Scottish Arts Council Touring Exhibition.
1971 'Modern Hangings from Scotland', English Speaking Union Gallery.
'Experimental Textiles', Camden Arts Centre, London.
1972 Annual Exhibition of the Society of Scottish Artists, Edinburgh.
'Tapestries from Edinburgh', Macrobert Centre, Stirling.
'Woven Structures', Camden Arts Centre, London.
1973 'Tapestries from Edinburgh', Macrobert Centre, Stirling.
'Scottish Crafts', Royal Scottish Museum, Edinburgh.
'Woven Structures', Camden Arts Centre, London.
Annual Exhibition of the Society of Scottish Artists, Edinburgh.
'Fifteen Weavers', British Crafts Centre, London.
'The Craftsman's Art', Victoria and Albert Museum, London.
'Aspects of Modern Crafts', Royal Scottish Museum, Edinburgh.
'Europalia '73', Brussels.
'Every Man a Patron', Design Council, London.
1974 1st World Craft Exhibition, Toronto.
1974 'Tapestries from Edinburgh', Stirling Gallery, Stirling.
1st International Miniature Textiles, London, Switzerland, New York.
Crafts Biennial, Scotland.
1975 1st Triennale of Tapestry, Lodz, Poland.
'The Need to Draw', Scottish Arts Council, Touring.
1976 2nd International Exhibition of Miniature Textiles, London.
1977 'British Craftsmen', Zurich (Atmosphere, London).
'Small Tapestries', Scottish Arts Council (Touring).
Scottish Tapestry, 'Loose Ends, Close Ties and Other Structures, The Way Ahead', Edinburgh College of Art.

MAJOR PUBLIC COMMISSIONS AND COLLECTIONS

Aberdeen: City Art Gallery and Regional Museum.
Edinburgh: Corporation Libraries and Museums Department.
Department of the Environment.
London and Edinburgh Insurance Company.
Midlothian County Council Offices.
Royal Scottish Museum.
St Cuthbert's Catholic Church.
Scottish Arts Council.

                Turnhouse Airport.
                Meadowbank Sports Centre.
Glasgow: Bearsden South Parish Church.
London: Victoria and Albert Museum.
                Heller Gallery.
                Crafts Advisory Committee.
                British Crafts Centre.
Motherwell and Wishaw Civic Centre.
Pennsylvania: Church of St John the Evangelist.
York University.
Dundee: Ninewells Hospital.
Melbourne: National Gallery of Victoria.
Zurich: Belle Rive Gallery.

MAJOR FEATURES AND PUBLICATIONS
'Archie Brennan' by Marigold Coleman, *Crafts* no. 8, May/June 1974.
'The Point about Weaving' by Fiona Adamczzwski, *Design* 307, July 1974.
'Archie Brennan' by Brian Beaumont-Nesbitt, *Connoisseur*, July 1974.

Geraldine Brock
'Badgers', Fiskerton Road, Southwell, Nottinghamshire, England.

GROUP EXHIBITIONS

Design Centres, London, Glasgow and Manchester.
1965 Weaving for Walls, Victoria and Albert Museum, London.
1970 Edinburgh, Scotland.
1972 Liverpool Polytechnic Weavers.
1973 Tapestry Exhibition, Camden Arts Centre, London.
1976 Sheila David Gallery, London.
1976 Textural Art Gallery, London.
1976 2nd International Exhibition of Miniature Textiles, Craft Centre, London.

PUBLIC COMMISSIONS AND COLLECTIONS

Lecture Theatre Building, Liverpool University, 1966.
Staff House, Liverpool University, 1968.
Trust Houses Forte, Post House Hotel, Otley, Leeds, 1972.
Department of the Environment.
Private collections.

Peter Collingwood
The Old School, Nayland, Colchester, Essex, England.

ONE-MAN EXHIBITIONS

1964 & 1973 British Crafts Centre, London.
1966 Building Centre, London.
1969 Victoria and Albert Museum, London (the first living weaver to have a one-man
     exhibition here).
1970 Roland Browse and Delbanco.
1970 Park Square Gallery, Leeds.
1971 & 1973 The Croneen Gallery, Sydney.
1971 St Cloud State College, USA.

1972 Oxford Gallery, Oxford.
1972 Heffers, Cambridge.
1973 Ashgate Gallery and Crafts Centre, London.
1974 Lantern Gallery, Ann Arbor, Michigan.
1975 Kunstindustrimuseet, Oslo.
1975 Kunstindustrimuseet, Copenhagen.
1975 Crafts Centre, London.
1975 Oxford Gallery, London.

GROUP EXHIBITIONS
Most general craft exhibitions from 1954 to date in UK including:
    1973 'The Craftsman's Art', Victoria and Albert Museum, London.
Also several travelling exhibitions in America, e.g.:
    1971 'Three British Weavers'.
    1972 'Fabrications'.
    1974 'The WCC Exhibition', Toronto.
1977 'Structure in Textile', Stedelijk Museum, Amsterdam.

PUBLIC COMMISSIONS AND COLLECTION
1956–69 Victoria and Albert Museum, London.
1962 Shell Centre, London.
1963 New Zealand House, London.
1964 Selwyn College, Cambridge.
1963, 1966, 1968 University of York.
1967 Metropolitan Cathedral, Liverpool.
1968 National and Grindlays, London.
1970 National Gallery of Melbourne.
1971 National Westminster Bank, Manchester.
1971 University of Liverpool.
1972 National Museum of Wales, Cardiff.
1972 Crafts Study Centre, Bath.
1973 Public Library, Welwyn Garden City.
1974 Philadelphia Museum of Art.
1975 Kunstindustrimuseet, Oslo and Copenhagen.
1975 Cooper Hewitt Museum, New York.
1976 Wellesley Office Park, Boston, Mass.
1976 Stedelijk Museum, Amsterdam.
1977 W.H. Smith, Head Office, London.
1977 Kuwait Embassy, London.

Bobbie Cox
Warren House, Dartington, Devon, England.

ONE-MAN EXHIBITION
1972 Exeter University Gallery.

GROUP EXHIBITIONS
1972 Vera Sherman travelling exhibitions including:
        Bermuda Summer Festival, Bermuda Arts Council, and
        Lincoln Cathedral 900 centenary.
1973 'The Craftsman and the Arts', Victoria and Albert Museum, London.
        Bath Festival.
        Arts South West.

Devon Guild of Craftsmen.
Guildford House Gallery, Surrey.
National Museum of Wales.
Textural Art Gallery, London W1.
British Crafts Centre.
'Crafts in Question', Whitworth Art Gallery, Manchester.
Craft Shop Ciderpress, Dartington.

WORKS IN PERMANENT COLLECTIONS
Devon County Council.
Yorkshire West Riding Collection.
Trust Houses Forte Ltd.
IBM.
Other private collections.

Fionna Geddes
Edinburgh College of Art, Lauriston Place, Edinburgh, Scotland.

ONE-MAN EXHIBITIONS
One-man show, Stirling Gallery, Stirling.
One-man show. Scottish Arts Council Coffee House, Charlotte Square, Edinburgh.
Fionna Geddes, New Work, New 57 Gallery, Edinburgh, 1977.

GROUP EXHIBITIONS
1973 Scottish Young Contemporaries.
1973–4 Royal Scottish Academy (Competitive examination finalist prizewinner 1973).
1974 'Among the Quiet Fibres' (Group Exhibition), Weavers Workshop, Edinburgh.
    Stowells Trophy, The Mall Gallery, London.
    S.T.V. Gateway Theatre, Festival Exhibition.
1974–5 Weavers Workshop Christmas Exhibition, Edinburgh.
1975 Scottish Tourist Board Group Exhibition, Birmingham.
    Society of Scottish Artists Annual Exhibition.
1975–6 'Trees' – Multi-Visual/Media Group Exhibition, Stirling Gallery, Stirling.
1976 'Printmakers as Photographers' Group Exhibition, Printmakers Workshop,
    Edinburgh.
    'Young Scottish Artists', Scottish Gallery, Edinburgh.
    New Acquisitions, Scottish Arts Council, Charlotte Square, Edinburgh.
    'Great British Crafts', Group Exhibition, Heal & Son Ltd, Tottenham Court Road,
    London.
    2nd International Exhibition of Miniature Textiles (tapestries), British Craft
    Centre, London (travelling to Aberdeen, Rotterdam).
    Amnesty International Festival Exhibition, Edinburgh.
    'Original Print 5' Travelling Exhibition, Printmakers Workshop, Edinburgh
    (Belfast, etc.).
    Society of Scottish Artists Annual Exhibition.
    Textural Art Gallery (Selected Group Opening Exhibition), Lansdowne Row,
    Berkeley Square, London.
1976–7 'Small Tapestries' – Scottish Arts Council Travelling Exhibition (Aberdeen
    opened).
1976–7 Printmakers Workshop Christmas Exhibition, Edinburgh.
1977 Scottish Tapestry 'Loose Ends, Close Ties and Other Structures – The Way
    Ahead', Edinburgh College of Art.

Scottish Arts Council.
Bank of Scotland.
York University.
Private collections in Britain.

Myriam Gilby
82 Princess Road, Buckhurst Hill, Essex, England.

ONE-MAN EXHIBITION
1970 One-man Exhibition (B.H. Corner Gallery, London).

GROUP EXHIBITIONS
1970 Contemporary Hangings: Mrs Vera Sherman, London (The Priory and Parish Church of St Margaret, Kings Lynn and elsewhere) (All Hallows on the Wall, London and elsewhere).
1970 'Modern British Hangings', Scottish Arts Council Gallery, Edinburgh and elsewhere.
1971–2 Inaugural Exhibition: 'Twenty-five British Weavers', Weavers Workshop Gallery, Edinburgh, 1971, and The Scottish Design Centre, Glasgow, 1972.
1972 Bermuda Arts Festival Exhibition: Mrs Vera Sherman, London (Bermuda 1972).
1972 Bath Festival Exhibition: Association of Guilds of Weavers, Spinners and Dyers, Victoria Art Gallery, Bath.
1972 1st Birthday Exhibition, Weavers Workshop Gallery, Edinburgh.
1973 'The Craftsman's Art': Crafts Advisory Committee, Victoria and Albert Museum, London.
1973 'Fifteen Weavers', The British Crafts Centre, London.
1975 Durham Cub Centre.
     Lincolnshire and South Humberside Cub, Usher Galley, Lincoln.
     Harlow Theatre Gallery.
1976 'Women at Work', Woburn Abbey.
     'Crafts in Question', Whitworth Gallery, Manchester.

Maureen Hodge
School of Tapestry, Edinburgh College of Art, Lauriston Place, Edinburgh, Scotland.

GROUP EXHIBITIONS
1963 The Arts Council of Great Britain (Scottish Committee), 'Leaded, Concreted and Sand-blasted Glass', Royal Scottish Academy, Edinburgh.
1965 2nd Biennale Internationale de la Tapisserie, Musée Cantonal des Beaux-Arts, Lausanne, Switzerland.
     'Weavers from the Dovecot Studio, Edinburgh', Whitworth Gallery, Manchester.
1967 3rd Biennale Internationale de la Tapisserie, Musée Cantonal des Beaux-Arts, Lausanne, Switzerland.
1968 Society of Scottish Artists Annual Exhibition, Royal Scottish, Academy, Edinburgh.
1969 'Tapestries and Ceramics Today', English Speaking Union, Edinburgh.
     S.S.A. Exhibition, R.S.A., Edinburgh.
     'Legacy of Scotland', Hammond Museum, North Salem, New York.
1970 'Modern British Hangings', Scottish Arts Council Gallery, Edinburgh.
     'Ten Years of Tapestry', Edinburgh College of Art (Festival Exhibition).
     S.S.A. Exhibition, R.S.A., Edinburgh.

1971 'Experimental Textiles', Camden Arts Centre, London.
   Inaugural Exhibition, Weavers Workshop, Edinburgh.
1972 'Woven Structures', Camden Arts Centre, London.
   S.S.A. Exhibition, R.S.A., Edinburgh.
1973 'Contemporary Scottish Hangings', Welsh Arts Council, Llantarnam Grange,
   Cumbrau New Town.
   'The Craftsman's Art', Victoria and Albert Museum, London.
   'L'Ecosse, La Femme et L'Art', Galerie des Ponchettes, Nice, France.
   'Fifteen Weavers', British Crafts Centre, London.
   'Europhalia – Hand and Machine', Brussels, Belgium.
   S.S.A. Exhibition, R.S.A., Edinburgh.
1974 'Tapestries from Edinburgh', British Crafts Centre, London.
   'Small Tapestries', Arts Council Coffee Shop, Edinburgh.
1974 'Tapestries from Edinburgh' (Three-man Show – Archie Brennan, Ellen Lenvik,
   Maureen Hodge), Stirling Gallery, Stirling.
   S.S.A. Exhibition, R.S.A., Edinburgh.
1975 1st Triennale of Textile Arts, Lodz, Poland (invited work).
   S.S.A. Exhibition, R.S.A., Edinburgh.
1976 'Miniatures in Fibre', Melbourne and Ararat, Australia.
   2nd International Exhibition of Miniature Textiles, British Craft Centre, London
   (then touring).
   S.S.A. Exhibition, R.S.A., Edinburgh.
   'Small Tapestries', Scottish Arts Council Travelling Show.
1977 Scottish Tapestry 'Loose Ends, Close Ties and Other Structures – The Way
   Ahead', Edinburgh College of Art.

PUBLIC COMMISSIONS AND COLLECTIONS
Scottish Arts Council Collection, Edinburgh.
Royal Scottish Museum Collection, Edinburgh.
Stirling University, Bridge of Allan Central Region.
Crafts Advisory Committee Collection, London.
Private collections in the United Kingdom, Australia and Canada.

Robert Mabon
Tanglewood, Wilton Lane, Jordans, Beaconsfield, Buckinghamshire, England.

ONE-MAN EXHIBITIONS
1968 British Crafts Centre.
1969 Peter Dingley Gallery, Stratford-upon-Avon.
1972, 1976 Salix Gallery, Windsor.

GROUP EXHIBITIONS
Work included in many mixed exhibitions in the UK, USA, Japan and Finland.

COMMISSIONS AND COLLECTIONS
Trust Houses Forte Ltd.
British National Export Council.
Reading Education Authority.
King Alfred's College, Winchester.
Dr Challoners School, Amersham.
Private collections in UK, USA, Japan and South Africa.

Fiona Mathison
School of Tapestry, Edinburgh College of Art, Lauriston Place, Edinburgh, Scotland.

GROUP EXHIBITIONS
1970 Blairlogie Arts Festival, Stirling.
    'Edinburgh Tapestries', Art College, Edinburgh.
    Society of Scottish Artists, Edinburgh.
1971 'Scottish Hangings', Edinburgh
    'Scottish Crafts', Royal Scottish Museum, Edinburgh.
1972 'Woven Structures', Camden Arts Centre, London.
    'Textile Diversions', Royal College of Art, London.
1973 Group Show, Stirling University, Stirling.
    'Aspects of Modern British Craft', Edinburgh.
    Work of Staff and Students of Royal College of Art, Japan.
    Society of Scottish Artists, Edinburgh.
    'Fifteen Weavers', British Crafts Centre, London.
    6th Biennale of Tapestry, Lausanne, Switzerland.
1974 Society of Scottish Artists, Edinburgh.
    Scottish Crafts Biennial, Edinburgh.
    'Tapestries from Edinburgh', Craft Centre, London.
    'Small Tapestries', Arts Council Coffee House, Edinburgh.
    One-Man Show, Arts Council Coffee House, Edinburgh.
    Group Show of Tapestry, Edinburgh Crafts, Edinburgh.
1975 Society of Scottish Artists, London.
    Society of Scottish Artists, Edinburgh.
1976 'Miniature in Fibre', Australia.
    Group Show, D.L.I. Museum, Durham.
    Society of Scottish Artists, Edinburgh.
    'Small Tapestries', Scottish Arts Council Travelling Exhibition.
1977 'The Way Ahead', Edinburgh College of Art, Edinburgh.

PUBLIC COMMISSIONS AND COLLECTIONS
Sick Children's Hospital, Edinburgh.
Tower Hotel, London.
First National Bank of Chicago, Edinburgh.
Private collections in Britain, USA and Australia.

Kathleen McFarlane
The Croft, Stody, Melton Constable, Norfolk, England.

ONE-MAN EXHIBITIONS
1973 Weavers Workshop, Edinburgh.
1974 Sunderland Civic Art Gallery.
1976 British Crafts Centre, London.

GROUP EXHIBITIONS
1970 Norwich Castle Museum.
1972 Weavers Workshop, Edinburgh.
1973 'Craftsman's Art', Victoria and Albert Museum, London.
1973 'Fifteen Weavers', British Crafts Centre, London.
1973 'Monarchy 1000', Bath.
1975 'Woven Works', Eastern Arts Association Touring Exhibition.
1975 Usher Gallery, Lincoln: Exhibition of weaving arranged by Lincolnshire Arts
    Association.

1975 'Weaving and Ceramics', Kettle's Yard, Cambridge.
1976 'Three Tapestry Weavers', D.L.I. Gallery, Durham.
1976 Minories, Colchester.
1976 Triennial Festival Exhibition, St Andrews Hall, Norwich.
1977 Gardner Centre, University of Sussex.
1977 Oxford Gallery, Oxford.

PUBLIC COMMISSIONS AND COLLECTIONS
1970 Altar frontal for St Margaret's Priory, King's Lynn.
1975 Leicestershire Education Authority.
1975 Norwich Castle Museum.
Private collectors.

Theo Moorman
'Stonebarrow', Tibbiwell Lane, Painswick, Gloucestershire, England.

ONE-MAN EXHIBITIONS
1963 One-man exhibition, The Manor House Ilkley.
      Theo Moorman: Tapestries and Church Fabrics.
1967 One-man exhibition, Queen Square Gallery, Leeds.
      One-man exhibition, Abbot Hall Art Gallery, Kendal.
1968 One-man exhibition, Goosewell Gallery, Menston.
1972 Oxford Gallery (recent works).
1975 Goosewell Gallery, Menston (recent works).
      Oxford Gallery (recent works).
      Royal Northern College of Music (recent works).
1976 Kettles Yard, Cambridge (recent small works).
      Art Alliance, Philadelphia (recent works)
      Park Square Gallery, Leeds (recent small works).

GROUP EXHIBITIONS
1955 Untitled group exhibition, City Art Gallery, Wakefield.
1962 'Artists Serve the Church', Herbert Art Gallery and Museum, Coventry.
1965 'Weaving for Walls', Victoria and Albert Museum, London.
1968 Mrs Vera Sherman, London: Contemporary Hangings (The Guildhall, Leicester,
      and elsewhere in Great Britain)
1968 Association of Guilds of Weavers, Spinners and Dyers: Woven Textiles '68,
      The Building Centre, London.
1969 'Church Embroidery and Handweaving of Today', York Minster.
1970 'New Work by Theo Moorman and Margaret Firth', Goosewell Gallery, Menston.
1970 Mrs Vera Sherman, London: Contemporary Hangings (The Priory and Parish
      Church of St Margaret, King's Lynn, and elsewhere in Great Britain).

PUBLIC COMMISSIONS AND COLLECTIONS
1956 Wakefield Cathedral.
1957, 1968, 1970 Manchester Cathedral.
1960 Gloucester Cathedral.
1961 St George's Church, Sheffield.
1962 St Etheldreda's Church, Fulham, London.
1962 St Mary's College, Cheltenham.
1963 Whiteland's College, Putney, London.
1964 Episcopalian Church, Aberfeldy, Perthshire.
1967 Dunscroft Church, near Doncaster.
1968 Agnes Stewart School, Leeds.

1969 Parish Church, Kendal.
1969 Cooper-Hewitt Museum of Design, New York.
1970 Cheltenham Parish Church.
1971 Middle Claydon Church, Bedfordshire.
1971 Oldbury Church, Warley, Worcestershire.
1975 Fitzwilliam College, Cambridge.
1975 Coughton Church, Warwickshire.
     Spokane, Washington, USA.
1977 Legal Offices of Scott B. Lukus.
     Hanley Castle Church, Worcestershire.

Alec Pearson
18 Greenlands, Cambridge, England.

EXHIBITIONS
1976 Joshua Taylor Gallery, Cambridge.
     Sheila David Gallery, London.
     The Minories, Colchester.
     The Textural Art Gallery, London.
1977 The Textural Art Gallery, London.
     The Bell Lane Gallery, Hertford.
     Philip Francis Gallery, Sheffield.
     Old Fire Engine House Gallery, Ely.

PUBLIC COMMISSIONS AND COLLECTIONS
Cambridge Institute of Education.
Joshua Taylor & Co., Cambridge.
Arthur Anderson & Co., London.
Two tapestries for the Guildhall School of Music and Drama new building in
Barbican, London.
Private collections in Britain, Brazil and USA.

Maggie Riegler
Dess Station Pottery, Kincardine O'Neil, Aberdeenshire, Scotland.

ONE-MAN EXHIBITION
1968 'Maggie Riegler, Recent Work', Civic Arts Centre, Aberdeen.

GROUP EXHIBITIONS
1967–9 Aberdeen Artists' Society annual exhibitions, Art Gallery and Regional
     Museum, Aberdeen.
1969 Society of Scottish Artists annual exhibition, Royal Scottish Academy,
     Edinburgh.
1969 The Scottish Arts Council: 'Modern Scottish Embroidery', Scottish Arts Council
     Gallery, Glasgow, and elsewhere in Scotland.
1969 'Tapestry and Ceramics Today', Edinburgh.
1970 'North East Artists', Compass Gallery, Glasgow.
1970 'Modern British Hangings', Scottish Arts Council, Edinburgh.
1972 'Three British Weavers', touring show, USA.
1973 'Craftsman's Art', Victoria and Albert Museum, London.
1973 'Fifteen Weavers', B.C.C., London.

1973 British Trades Mission, Vancouver, B.C.
1973 'Aspects of Modern British Crafts', Royal Scottish Museum, Edinburgh.
1974 Group Show of Tapestry, Edinburgh Crafts Gallery.
1974 Selected and exhibited in 1st Scottish Crafts Biennial, Edinburgh.
1975 'Five Scottish Craftsmen', Festival Exhibition, Edinburgh.
1976 Group Show, Durham Light Infantry Museum and Arts Centre.
1976 Scottish Tapestry retrospective exhibition 1960–76, Edinburgh College of Art.
1977 'Small Tapestries', Scottish Arts Council, touring show.

Sax Shaw
25 Howe Street, Edinburgh, Scotland.

ONE-MAN EXHIBITIONS
1955 Edinburgh Tapestry Company Ltd: Dovecot Tapestries: Sax Shaw – The Scottish
     Gallery, Aitken Dott & Son, Edinburgh.
1959 One-man exhibition, Ian Clarkson Gallery, Edinburgh.
1962 One-man exhibition, University Exhibition Hall, University of Exeter.
1963 Exhibition of Tapestry, Lane Gallery, Bradford.
1963 Exhibition of Tapestry, Art Gallery and Museum, Keighley.
1967 Four one-man exhibitions, Richard Demarco Gallery, Edinburgh.
1967 Tapestries by Sax Shaw, Graves Art Gallery, Sheffield.
1968 Tapestry by Sax Shaw: Lane Gallery, Bradford; Farnley Hall, Otley; Goosewell
     Gallery, Menston.
     The Institute of Directors, The Crafts Centre of Great Britain and The Scottish
     Craft Centre: Skill (Goldsmiths' Hall, London and elsewhere in Great Britain).
1976 Exhibition of watercolours in Stiegal's Gallery, Edinburgh.

GROUP EXHIBITIONS
1959–60 'British Artist Craftsmen', An Exhibition of Contemporary Work circulated
     by the Smithsonian Institution, Washington DC.
1962 The Scottish Committee of the Arts Council of Great Britain: 'The Jubilee of the
     Dovecot Tapestries 1912–62', Edinburgh.
1962 'Artists Serve the Church', Herbert Art Gallery and Museum, Coventry.
1963 'Experimental Tapestries by Scottish Weavers', Institute of Advanced
     Architectural Studies, University of York.
1965 The Grail, Edinburgh: 'Sacred-Art', Adam House, University of Edinburgh.
1966 'Tapestries from the Dovecot Studio, Edinburgh', Lane Gallery, Bradford;
     Art Gallery and Museum, Keighley.

PUBLIC COMMISSIONS AND COLLECTIONS
Several stained-glass windows and mural decorations.
Tapestries in:
1955 Bearsden church, Glasgow.
1955 Rolls Royce Guest House, Hillington.
1956 Martin's Bank, Tottenham Court Road, London.
1957–8 Coventry Cathedral.
1958 Glasgow Cathedral.
1958 New Chapel, Warriston Crematorium, Edinburgh.
1964 Designed the choir gowns for St Giles.
1966–7 St Kentigern's Church, Edinburgh.
1967 Parish Church, Corstorphine (woven by the Edinburgh Tapestry Co. Ltd., 1967).
1970 St John's Church, Edinburgh.
1970 Tapestry – 'Witherslack' for Mrs Stanley, Grangemouth on Sands.

1971 Netherlea Church, Glasgow – 2-light window.
1971 Hyndland Parish Church, Glasgow – 3-light Creation window.
1972 Salvesen Tapestry, Edinburgh – 'Re-Entry'.
1973 Window for the abbey church, North Berwick.
1973 Dunfermline – 3-light window – now destroyed by fire.
1975 Carmargue panel for Liverpool University Veterinary College.
1977 Currently working on baptistry window at Prestonpans.
Private collections.

Unn Sönju
School of Creative Art and Design, Leeds Polytechnic, Leeds, England.

ONE-MAN EXHIBITIONS
1971 Holst Halvorsens Kunsthandel A/s, Oslo.
1972 Galleri Kim, Stavanger, Norway.
1973 Northern Artists Gallery Ltd, Leeds.
     Huddersfield Polytechnic Gallery.
1974 Mid-Pennine Association for the Arts, Blackburn.
1975 Sheila David Gallery, London.
1977 Kunsternes Hus, Oslo.
     Kunstforeningen, Stavanger.
     Bergens Kunstforeningen, Bergen.
     Trondhjems Kunstforening, Trondheim, Norway.

GROUP EXHIBITIONS
1966 Queens Square Gallery, Leeds.
1967 'Then and Now', Institute Gallery, Leeds.
1968 'Three Aspects of Tapestry', Institute Gallery, Leeds.
1969 Senior Common Room, Leeds University.
1970 Cochran Gallery, Washington, USA.
     Richmond Hill Gallery, London.
     'Modern British Hangings', Edinburgh Festival.
1971 Kunstgalleri, Stavanger, Norway.
1972 'New Tapestries for Leeds', Retford, Nottinghamshire.
     Weavers Workshop, Summer Exhibition, Edinburgh.
     Statens Höstutstilling, Oslo, Norway.
     Weavers Workshop, Edinburgh.
1973 National Craft Exhibition, Victoria and Albert Museum, London.
     'New British Hangings', Edinburgh.
     1st British International Drawing Biennial, Middlesbrough.
     Statens Höstutstilling, Oslo, Norway.
1974 'Woven Hangings', City Art Gallery, Wakefield.
     'A-Priori', Cartwright Hall Museum, Bradford.
     'Tapestries from the Fine Art Department, Leeds Polytechnic', Weavers
     Workshop, Edinburgh.
     Sommer Utstilling, Kunstnernes Hus, Oslo, Norway.
     Statens Höstutstilling, Oslo, Norway.
1975 Tekstilgruppen i U.K.S., Stavanger Kunstforening.
     'kvinnen og kunsten', Kunsteres Hus, Oslo.
     'Norsk tekstilkunst idag', Kunstforeningen, Oslo.
1976 U.K.S. Varuistilling, Kunsternes Hus, Oslo.
1976–7 Nordisk Tekstiltriennale shown Denmark, Sweden, Iceland, Finland, Faroes,
     Norway.
1976 Galleri Buttekvern, Brumundal, Norway.

Ann Sutton
Parnham House, Beaminster, Dorset, England.
Parnham House is open 10–5 Wednesdays and Sundays, April to October.

ONE-MAN EXHIBITIONS
1969 'Ann Sutton, Textiles', Craft Centre, London.
1970 One-man print show, Victoria and Albert Museum Circulation.
1975 'Ann Sutton, Textiles', Craft Centre, London.
1976 One-man show, 'Collection', Birmingham.
1977 Ann Sutton Exhibition, Dodson Bull Interiors, Barbican, London.

GROUP EXHIBITIONS
1958 'Nine Artists', Hove Museum.
1959 Red Rose Guild of Craftsmen, Whitworth Museum, Manchester.
    Arts and Crafts Exhibition Society and later as Society of Designer Craftsmen.
1965 'Weaving for Walls', Victoria and Albert Museum, London.
1965 'Decorative Objects', Bear Lane Gallery, Oxford.
1968 'Woven Textiles '68', Building Centre, London.
1968 'Ten Designer Craftsmen', Design Centre, London.
1970 Design '70 with J. Makepeace & G. Baldwin, Oxford Gallery.
1970 Beutlich/Collingwood/Sutton at the Croneen Gallery, Sydney, Australia.
1970 'Modern British Hangings', Scottish Arts Council, Edinburgh Festival.
1972 'Woven Structures', Camden Arts Centre, London.
1973 'The Craftsman's Art', Victoria and Albert Museum, London.
1976 'Wall Hangings', Usher Gallery, Lincoln.
1976 'Ceramics/Textiles', Gardner Centre, University of Sussex.

PUBLIC COMMISSIONS AND COLLECTIONS
Victoria and Albert Museum: 20 pieces (1964, 1967, 1970).
National Museum of Wales: 16 pieces (1966, 1972).
Oxford City and County Museum (1967).
City of Leeds Museum and Art Gallery, Lotherton Hall (1976).

PUBLIC COMMISSIONS AND COLLECTIONS
Crew Law Courts (light fitment).
Company Record Office, Cardiff (2 hangings).
Jesus Centre, Birmingham (2 hangings).
Work in numerous private collections.

With their permission, the addresses of artists' studios have been included. Visitors are generally welcome, but *never* without prior appointment.

Bibliography

Books concerned with fine-art weaving

Albers, Anni, *On Weaving*, Studio Vista, 1966.

Constantine, Mildred and Larsen, Jack, *Beyond Craft, the Art Fabric*, Van Nostrand Reinhold, New York, 1973.

Jarry, Madeleine, *La Tapisserie, Art du XXieme Siècle*, Office de Levie, Paris, 1974 (text in French).

Kaufmann, Ruth, *The New American Tapestry*, Reinhold Book Corporation, New York, 1968.

Kuenzi, André, *La Nouvelle Tapisserie*, Bonvent, 1973 (text in French).

Waller, Irene, *Thread, an Art Form*, Studio Vista, London, 1973; entitled *Designing with Thread*, Viking, New York.

Waller, Irene, *Textile Sculptures*, Studio Vista, London, 1977; Taplinger, New York.

Waller, Irene, *Knots and Netting*, Studio Vista, London, 1976; Taplinger, New York.

Books concerned with technical aspects of weaving
(referred to within the text)

Beutlich, Tadek, *The Technique of Woven Tapestry*, Batsford, London; Watson-Guptill, New York, 1967.

Collingwood, Peter, *Techniques of Rug Weaving*, Faber & Faber, 1967.

Collingwood, Peter, *The Techniques of Sprang*, Faber & Faber, 1974.

Davenport, Elsie, *Your Handspinning*, Sylvan Press, 1953.

Davenport, Elsie, *Your Yarndyeing*, Sylvan Press, 1955.

Davenport, Elsie, *Your Handweaving*, Sylvan Press, 1970.

d'Harcourt, Raoul, *Textiles of Ancient Peru and their Techniques*, University of Washington Press, 1974.

Gilby, Myriam, *Free Weaving*, Pitman, 1976.

Hooper, Luther, *Hand-loom Weaving*, Pitman, 1920.

Kirby, Mary, *Designing on the Loom*, Studio Publications, 1955; Dover, 1975.

Mairet, Ethel, *Vegetable Dyes*, Faber & Faber, 1916.

Mairet, Ethel, *Handweaving and Education*, Faber & Faber, 1942.

Mairet, Ethel, *Handweaving Today*, Faber & Faber, 1939.

Straub, Marianne, *Hand Weaving and Cloth Design*, Pelham, 1977.

Sutton, Ann, and Holtom, Pat, *Tablet Weaving*, Batsford, 1975.

Tovey, John, *The Technique of Weaving*, Batsford, 1965.

Tovey, John, *Weaves and Pattern Drafting*, Batsford, 1969.

Photograph Acknowledgments

Manor Studios, Hassocks, Sussex   1.2
Guardian Newspapers   1.15, 7.1
John Wilkie, Edinburgh   2.2, 2.7, 8.3–8.6, 10.2, 10.5
Reg Cox, Liverpool   3.2
Charles Seeley, Woodbridge, Suffolk   4.2–4.7, 4.9
Tom Scott, Edinburgh   6.8, 8.2
Mark Gerson, London   7.2, 7.7, 7.8
J.R. Jameson, Beaconsfield, Bucks   9.5
N.F. Large   12.2, 12.3, 12.6
Entwhistle, Thorpe & Co Ltd, Dukinfield, Cheshire   12.4
Jones Photography, Gloucester   12.5
Foto Lore Bermbach, Dusseldorf   13.2–13.4, 13.11
Lloyd Phillips   13.1, 13.6
Maureen MacLeod   17.3, 17.4
Sam Sawdon   17.5, 17.11
Hylton Warner & Co Ltd   17.7
. . . and the artists

Index

Abakanowicz, Magdalena 18, 19, 21, 74, 89
Abstract Expressionism 86
Adams, Alice 18
Akle technique 116
Albers, Anni 16
Albers, Josef 16
All Saints College 96
Amaral, Olga de 18, 21
Antilla, Eva 8
Association of Guilds of Weavers, Spinners and Dyers 11, 15, 16, 18, 60
Arts Council of Great Britain 90
Art and Craft Exhibition of 1888 8
Arts and Crafts Movement of 1861 8

Bachelor of Arts, Textiles 13
Banbury School of Art 126
Barker, Mary 16
Barlow & Jones Ltd 13
Bath Academy of Art 50
Baudouin, Pierre 30
Bauhaus, The 8, 12, 13, 16, 20
Beales, Percy and Rita 11
Berlin Modeschule der Stadt 12
Beutlich, Tadek 6, 14, 15, 16, 17, 20, 22–9, 86, 96
Binding technique 38, 58
Breed, Hilda 16
Brennan, Archie 6, 17, 19–21, 30–7, 66, 78
'Britain Can Make It' Exhibition 12
British Crafts Centre 18, 20, 22, 89, 122
Brock, Geraldine 38–41
Buic, Jagoda 18, 74
Butrymowicz, Zofia 18

Camberwell School of Art 14, 22, 72
Camden Arts Centre 19
Cardiff College of Art 120
Central College of Art 11, 13, 16, 72, 90
Ceramics 74
City and Guilds of London 12
Collingwood, Peter 6, 10, 14–17, 20, 22, 42–9
Cotton Board 122
Corduroy weave 45
Coper, Hans 14, 15, 47
Cox, Bobbie 20, 21, 50–5
Crafts 20

'Crafts '57' Exhibition 18
'Craftsman's Art' Exhibition 15, 20, 88, 124
Crafts Advisory Committee 19, 20
Crochet 38, 88
Croydon School of Art 120
Cruickshank, Ronald 19, 30

Dartington Hall 11, 50
Darwin, Sir Robin 12
Davenport, Elsie 11
Design Centre 12, 15, 42
Deutsche Werkstatten 12
Digswell House Arts Centre 42
Di Mare, Dominic 18, 74
Diploma in Industrial Design 12
Diploma in Art and Design 13
Dorn, Marion 9
Double-weaving 74, 122

Edinburgh College of Art 19, 21, 30, 31, 33, 66, 78, 80, 110
Edinburgh Festival 19
Edinburgh Tapestry Company 19, 30, 33, 66, 80, 110
Edinburgh Weavers Company 17
'Experimental Textiles' Exhibition 19

'Festival of Britain' 12
Finger-shedding 98
Frame weaving 74
Frankenthaler, Helen 86
Free shuttling 92
French Tapestry Exhibition 18, 22
Frost, Terry 114

Geddes, Fionna 19, 21, 56–9
Gilby, Myriam 20, 21, 60–5
Gill, Eric 9, 42
Golden Targe 30
Goldsmith's College 60
Gottlieb, Adolph 86
Grays School of Art 102
Grabowski Gallery 14, 18, 74
Greggs of Stockport 10
Grierson, Ronald 9
Griffiths, Hugh 15
Griffiths, Joyce 10, 15
Guermonprez, Trude 18

Hallman, Ted 18
Hardingham, Martin 13, 19
Hawkes, Jacquetta 11
Heal & Son Ltd 9, 15, 42, 90
Helios Ltd 13
Hicks, Sheila 18–21
Hindson, Alice 11
Hodge, Maureen 6, 19–21, 35, 66–71
Holtom, Pat 126
Homerton College 96
Hornsey College of Art 13
Huddersfield School of Art 110
Hudson, Tom 114
Hunter, Alec 17
Hurle, Ruth 12, 16, 60
Hürlimann, Heinz Otto 13

Industrial Revolution 7
Invesalo, Kirsti 38
Itten, Johannes 8

Jarosnyczka, Ewa 18

Kensington Weavers 11
Kingston School of Art 16
Kirby, Mary 16
Klee, Paul 8
Knitting 38, 123, 124
Knotting 38, 58, 88, 103

Lancaster Carpet Co 40
Lashing technique 56
Lausanne Biennales of Tapestry 18, 19, 20, 30, 79
Leach, Bernard 10
Leischner, Margaret 12, 13, 14, 17
Leeds College of Art 96, 114
Liberty & Co 9
Liverpool College of Art 38, 40
London Building Centre 14, 18
London School of Weaving 11
Lurçat, Jean 110

Måås-Fjetterström, Märta 8
Mabon, Robert 21, 72–7
Macrogauze weave 45
Macramé 74
Marimekko 102
Mairet, Ethel 9, 13–15, 20, 22, 42
Mairet, Philip 9
Marini, Mario 17
Martin, Kenneth 122

Mathison, Fiona 19, 21, 78–83
Maxwell, George and John 15
Miniature Textiles Exhibitions 20, 22, 126
Milan Triennale 18
'Modern British Hangings' 15, 19
'Modern American Wallhangings' 18
'Modern Hangings from Scotland' 19
Moore, Henry 84, 86, 92
Moorman, Theo 6, 16, 17, 20, 21, 90–5
Moorman weaving technique 92
Motherwell, Robert 86
Morton Sundour 17
Morton, Alistair 17, 20, 42
Morris, William 7, 8, 11, 14, 19
McFarlane, Kathleen 6, 18, 20, 84–9

National Diploma in Design 12, 13
Netting 60
Newcastle College of Art 56
Newcastle University 84
Nicholson, Ben 17, 42, 92

'Objects USA' 19
Overshot weave 92
Overtwisting 77
Owidzka, Jolanta 18

Painting 58, 86, 96, 113
Parrott, Alice 18
Pasmore, Victor 84
Pauli, Pierre 30
Peacock, Elizabeth 10, 11
Pearson, Alec 21, 96–100

Pepler, Marion 9
Plaiting 38
Primavera Gallery 9

Queen Elizabeth College 13

Regent Street Polytechnic 60
Riegler, Maggie 20, 102–9
Reigate School of Art 11
Resin bonding 56
Royal College of Art 12–16
Royal Designers for Industry 10, 14
Royal Society of Arts 10, 12, 14, 38, 133
Rural Industries Bureau 13
Rya technique 38, 124
Ryggen, Hannah 114

Sadley, Wojciech 18, 74
Sawyer, Barbara 10, 22, 42
Scottish Arts Council 15, 19, 35, 56
Scottish Tapestry Exhibition 19
Seagrott, Margaret 16
Shaft-switching weave technique 46
Shaw, Sax 17, 19, 21, 30, 31, 110–13
Sir John Cass School of Art 16
Smith, Richard 93
Sönju, Unn 20–2, 114–19
Spencer, Stanley
Sprang technique 46
Spinning 50, 64
Straub, Marianne 10, 13, 17
Stanhope Institute 60
Still, Clifford 86

Sussex College of Art 20
Sutherland, Graham 19
Sutton, Ann 6, 16, 18, 20, 120–7

Tamesa Fabrics 14
Tapestry weaving 22, 38, 50, 52, 66, 72, 74, 76, 78, 82, 87, 88, 96, 98, 110
Tawney, Lenore 18
Taylor, Walter 11, 90
Thubron, Harry 114
Tovey, John 16
Trent Polytechnic 40
Twisting technique 38

Victoria and Albert Museum 14, 15, 18, 20, 66, 133

Walker Phillips, Mary 18
Warner & Sons Ltd 8, 13, 14, 17, 90
'Weaving for Walls' Exhibition 14, 18
Weavers Journal 16, 20
Weavers Workshop 19
Wilkinson, Dorothy 11
Whitechapel Art Gallery 16, 19
'Woven Textiles '68' 14, 18
'Woven Forms' Exhibition 18
'Woven Structures' Exhibition 19
Wrapping technique 88
Wright, Austin 92

Zachai, Dorian 18
Zeisler, Clare 18
Zurich School of Applied Arts 13